Fit to Work

PADDY O'BRIEN was born in Gateshead in 1953. She runs a personnel training consultancy and works in a wide variety of organizations, from petrochemical to opera companies, voluntary organizations to universities. In the course of her work she has observed the impact of physical fitness on output and performance. She is a qualified yoga teacher and black belt martial artist, and has put together a series of methodical, easy-to-follow programmes which span the spectrum from zero fitness to athlectic prowess, to provide fitness choices for today's workers.

Sheldon Business Books

Sheldon Business Books is a list which exists to promote and facilitate the adoption of humane values and equal opportunities integrated with the technical and commercial expertise essential for successful business practice. Both practical and theoretical issues which challenge today's workforce will be explored in jargon-free, soundly researched books.

The first titles in the series are:
Taking the Macho Out of Management
   by Paddy O'Brien
How to Succeed in Psychometric Tests
   by David Cohen
Making Change Work for You
   by Alison Hardingham

Paddy O'Brien **Fit to Work**

Sheldon Business Books

First published in Great Britain 1993
Sheldon Press, SPCK, Marylebone Road, London NW1 4DU

© Paddy O'Brien 1993

All rights reserved. No part of this book may be reproduced or transmitted in any form or by any means, electronic or mechanical, including photocopying, recording, or by any information storage and retrieval system, without permission in writing from the publisher.

Disclaimer: the author and publisher disclaim any liability or loss, personal or otherwise, resulting from the procedures described in this book.

British Library Cataloguing-in-Publication Data
A catalogue record for this book is available from the British Library
ISBN 0-85969-680-4

Typography by Daniel Edwards
Photoset by Deltatype Ltd, Ellesmere Port, Cheshire
Printed in Great Britain at The University Press, Cambridge

Contents

   1 Introduction
   5 Project One
  47 Project Two
  79 Project Three
106 Project Four
119 Further Reading
121 Index

Introduction

This is a book for anyone who feels they would like genuinely to be fit to work. There is a growing body of evidence that the performance of people in high-pressure jobs is improved by those people taking regular exercise. There is also a growing cultural sense that it is preferable: it is admirable, interesting, attractive, sensible, to be fit and feel well rather than to be unfit and feel terrible. This marks a difference, a new step, from the panic culture of the 1980s where credibility could be established by looking and feeling wrecked ('I'm so high-powered, I'm so important, I never get a chance to stop; I fuel it all with alcohol, cigarettes, uppers, high-fat food') to a more holistic view in the 1990s where it is part of commanding respect and having self-respect to be well and strong.

This book, then, is for anybody who has a sense that they would like to get themselves organized to feel better all of the time. Physical exercise is only part of the picture in this enterprise. We need to address ourselves to other issues, such as our ability to handle stress, how we choose to eat and drink, how we make choices about smoking, and we also need to look in the widest sense at how we make career choices – for instance, how we assess *all* the implications of a promotion or a move, and how we manage career turbulence like redundancy or takeover, increasingly challenges *anyone* may have to face in these multiple recessionary times. Some of the growing database concerned with connecting fitness with performance gives us a picture of the key benefits we can expect.

Decision-making
   Executives who work out regularly are actually better decision-makers. Dr Gabriel Salvendy (of Purdue University) tested decision-making capabilities of 80 people over a nine-month period of time. At the end of the test period, the fitness

level of the exercisers had risen 22%, while the ability to make complex decisions had risen 70% over that of the non-exercisers.

(Robert Brosmer, Deborah Waldren, *Health and High Performance*, 1991)

Absence/presence at work
Dupont reduced absenteeism by 47% over six years for its corporate fitness programme participants.
(D. W. Edington, Health Behaviours, March 1992)

General Electric found that employees who exercised were absent from work 45% fewer days than employees who did not.
(Nancy Coe Bailey, Business and Health, November 1990)

Improved output
When compared to the average office worker whose efficiency decreases 50% for the final two hours of the working day, the exercise adherents worked at full efficiency all day. This amounted to a 12.5% increase in productivity.
(*Company Sponsored Employee Fitness Programs*, Association for Fitness in Business, 1991)

Reduced error rate
Mental performance after exercise was significantly better in the physically fit than in the non-fit. Fit workers committed 27% fewer errors on tasks involving concentration and short-term memory as compared to unfit workers.
(Hans Sjoberg, Ergonomics, 1983)

These compelling and measurable benefits are ours for the taking if we are prepared to put the steady investment into ourselves, our fitness and well-being, that we need to get them. The type of shortfall in fitness which we may be looking at is indicated in The Allied Dunbar National Fitness Survey for 1992:

Although 80% of the population believe themselves to be fit, one third of men and two thirds of women are unable to continue walking at a reasonable pace (about 3 m.p.h.) up a 1 in 20 slope without becoming breathless, finding it physically demanding and having to slow down or stop.

48% of men and 40% of women are overweight and the numbers have increased from 39% and 32% since 1980.

In other words we are often not as fit as we think we are, and, as a nation, are increasingly heavier than we should be. Our use of cars, our sedentary jobs, our workaholism (no time, no energy left for exercise) are all to blame. The good news, however, starts here. It *is* possible to make choices and make changes at an individual level without large investment in money, with only moderate investment in time, and with commonsense and goodwill, which can radically change things in our own lives. Following the projects in this book can be a positive and structured way to make those changes for you.

A real sense of how the intellect and emotions link in to muscular, skeletal, and organic well-being is the key to what we are looking for. Once you truly inhabit your body – rather than feeling it is a nuisance, a liability, the wrong size, the wrong shape, not strong enough, not sexy enough, whatever – you have access to a wonderful flow of energy, a clear thinking process, and a very solid, sensual, physical delight purely in being alive. This may sound like an inflated claim, but it is, if anything, an understatement, as anyone who has rediscovered their body in their adult life will testify.

The way the book works is to help you to focus on where you are now and how you want to change through three twelve-week projects, which are at beginning, intermediate, and advanced levels of fitness, well-being, and relaxation techniques. Even if you feel fairly fit when you begin the projects, start at the intermediate rather than the advanced level so that you have a chance to assimilate all the different aspects of the programme. Questionnaires help you to build your own programme and weekly charts help you to do the actual work and have a sense of your own progress. There is a fourth project which is all about using your bodily strength and awareness, and your good stress-handling and relaxation techniques, to manage pressurizing situations. For example, if you travel a great deal there are

4 Fit To Work

physical and emotional challenges to deal with; or you might be going through specific physical experiences like pregnancy or the menopause or recovering from serious illness; or you might be holding down a difficult job while surviving a marital breakdown or a bereavement; or you might lose your job and be dealing with all the financial and emotional fallout from that. The knowledge and insights, as well as the physical fitness, which you gain from the other three projects can be fine-tuned to meet those pressures as and when they arise.

The emphasis in these projects is all about starting from where you are now. We are all familiar with the humiliating business of going to an exercise class and it becoming apparent within moments that one is the only person who actually *needs* to be there: that everybody else is entirely fit already. Many of us, too, have made our hesitant way into a gym clad in a long, loose and, we hope, not too-revealing T-shirt, to find the place populated by huge men, their pectoral muscles peeping out of their cut-away vests, and fierce looking nymphs wearing all-over condoms, briskly shifting enormous stacks of weights. At which point, many of us make our hesitant way straight back out again.

It really does not matter if you have not done any proper exercise since your last game of football or netball at school, if you are jet-lagged and over-lunched and burned out. You can start here, with Project One; take your own time, and gradually rebuild your awareness and pride in your physical self, your emotional resilience, and your fitness and strength. Before long you will be enjoying the journey. Good luck!

Project One

This Project is the place to start if you have not done any regular exercise for more than six months, enough to make you both break out into a sweat and mobilize your body in more ways than that needed for everyday sitting, standing, and walking – i.e. exercise which makes you stretch, twist, bend, and have a wide range of leg and arm movement. (If you regularly play a sport or attend a class which causes you to do all of those things, you can begin at Project Two). What we are trying to do in this Project is to build a fitness base. It is a process of rediscovery, of reaffiliating yourself with that most precious asset, your body.

Answer the Questionnaire first, to give yourself a focus on how your body is now, how you feel about it, and what changes, at a first think through of the subject, you would like to see in your physical self. Also consider the other aspects of the programme, like how well you sleep, how well you handle stress, and so forth. Then allow yourself time to read through the discussion of each of the five parts of your Project One Programme: cardiovascular, toning, flexibility, stress management, and lifestyle. Where there are exercises to undertake, instructions for those exercises are set out. When you come to start doing your weekly charts, you will find the exercises have a number in brackets next to them: that is the page number on which you can find the instructions for that exercise, in case you have forgotten precisely how to do it.

Once you feel you have absorbed the thinking and information in the five sections, move onto the weekly charts. Fill them in every day and allow yourself to notice and enjoy any progress. If things do not go so well, do not get depressed. If you have a bad day or a bad week where you cannot motivate yourself or you overeat or feel disheartened, do not let it bog you down. It really does not matter. A steady, sustained effort will make an enormous difference to your well-being, and the odd off-day will not destroy that progress. Look on the time you put in as an investment that will grow geometrically – or like compound interest. In other words, if you exercise and fulfil the other parts of the weekly programme on two days a week, it will do you more than twice as much good as exercising and fulfilling the programme on one day a week. Gradually you 'store' more and more fitness and well-being in your body. It is a beneficent (the opposite of a vicious) circle: the better you feel, the more you have an interest in feeling good, so the less you are inclined to let your exercise session get crowded out of your day, or binge on food, alcohol or nicotine.

Questionnaire: Where are we starting from?

Tick whichever statement applies to you most closely in each question. Making that choice will give you something to think about regarding the issue dealt with in that question. Make a note of the thoughts that occur to you in the comment box. For example, if in question 1 you put a tick in the box next to 'ran 2km' you might write down, 'I'm confident I can do a short sprint if I had to, but I know I'd have trouble running for more than a few seconds.' If you ticked 'I'm not sure . . .', you might put, 'It's a surprise to realize that I have no idea whether I can walk at speed or run much at all; I just never consider such things.' Do not be afraid to note down any emotional reactions you have – for instance, you might want to write, 'I had to tick "ran up a flight of stairs" on this question, and that really upsets me. I used to be so fit three or four years ago, I feel really ashamed to confront the fact that I could barely run up the stairs now.' Those feelings are very important because they can, ironically enough, be the stumbling block which stops you getting fit again. In some ways it is even harder for a person who was very fit, but has let it all go, to get into a pair of shorts and start all over again, faced at every turn with the contrast between what they used to be able to do and where they have to start from now, than it is for a person who has never been fit, to make a start, because everything, for them, is progress.

Remember, with this programme, you start from where you

are now. We have all lived the sort of lives we needed to to survive so far. There is nothing to be ashamed of in that; on the contrary, we need to celebrate ourselves, our inventiveness and resilience, our ability to stay alive. If we want to make some changes now, fine. There is no need for any self-flagellation on the topic of having become heavy, or run down, or addicted, or any of those things. There is just a need to understand where we are coming from and why, and what is feasible and practical and desirable in the future. Repairing and rediscovering one's relationship with one's own body and well-being, is, as will become clear to you the further you get into it, in fact a profound act of self-development.

With those things in mind, be as thoughtful as you like and enjoy yourself with this self-diagnostic questionnaire.

1   **I would get out of breath if I**

☐ walked up a flight of stairs.

☐ ran up a flight of stairs.

☐ ran 50 yards to catch a bus or train.

☐ ran 2 km.

☐ I could manage any of those things easily.

☐ I'm not sure what it would take to make me breathless.

Comment . . .

2   **When I think about how much fat and how much muscle there is in my body I feel**

☐ the distribution is about right.

☐ there is too much fat in specific areas.

☐ there is too much fat all over.

☐ I feel a bit tight and muscle-bound.

☐ I feel rather thin and weak.

☐ I feel very slim but it is a constant effort to remain so.

Comment . . .

3 Generally speaking my digestive system

☐ works well.

☐ has occasional problems.

☐ is a worry to me.

☐ reacts violently to stress.

☐ never crosses my mind.

Comment . . .

4 Generally speaking I sleep

☐ very peacefully.

☐ too long.

☐ nowhere near enough.

☐ in a disturbed pattern because of small children.

☐ in a disturbed pattern because I have to get up to pee.

☐ patchily because of worry.

☐ very little because of chronic insomnia.

Comment . . .

5 I would describe food and eating as

☐ a pleasure.

☐ a constant worry.

☐ a time-consuming nuisance.

☐ an effort because I have to plan it all.

☐ an important part of work-related socializing.

Comment . . .

6 **Regarding my physical flexibility**
   ☐ I can easily touch my toes.
   ☐ I have niggling (or serious) back or joint problems.
   ☐ I have no idea whether I am flexible or not.
   ☐ I do stretching exercises at least twice a week.
   ☐ I suffer from very tight neck and shoulder muscles.

Comment . . .

7 **Alcohol for me is**
   ☐ an essential part of every day.
   ☐ an essential part of every weekend.
   ☐ an occasional recreation.
   ☐ not part of my life at all.
   ☐ a real worry because of my growing dependency on it.

Comment . . .

8 **I smoke**
   ☐ no cigarettes at all.
   ☐ a few cigarettes per week.
   ☐ a few cigarettes per day.
   ☐ over 20 cigarettes per day.
   ☐ over 40 cigarettes per day.

Comment . . .

10 *Fit To Work*

9 **I take the following drugs on prescription for the following conditions . . .**

   Comment: . . .

10 **I use the following drugs (other than nicotine or alcohol) recreationally . . .**

   Comment: . . .

11 **The tone and strength of my abdominal muscles is**
   ☐ fair.
   ☐ terrible.
   ☐ excellent.
   ☐ weak but improving.
   ☐ I have no idea.

   Comment . . .

12 **Generally speaking**
   ☐ I like my body.
   ☐ I try to ignore my body.
   ☐ I feel unhappy about my body.
   ☐ I feel proud of my body.
   ☐ I feel mystified by my body.

   Comment . . .

OVERALL REVIEW

I was pleasantly surprised to notice:

I was shocked by:

I've noticed the following information about myself:

I have the following new insights about my own feelings:

What I most want to achieve is:

Overall I now feel:

You will notice that with this questionnaire you do not add scores up and then get told something about yourself. Although such questionnaires are fun, they do not help you to do the essential work of getting to know yourself *for* yourself. Your 'Overall Review' at the end of the questionnaire gives you a chance to collect your thoughts. If those thoughts are difficult to take, do not despair. This is your starting place for making a difference to the unique person that is you. If your thoughts are positive, that is great. You have the energy of that positivity to take you forwards.

Let us take some time now to discuss the five fitness elements: cardiovascular work, flexibility, toning, stress management and relaxation techniques, and total lifestyle, and learn the specific exercises we need to learn to move onto the Week One Chart.

Cardiovascular fitness

Aerobic or cardiovascular capacity is the ability of the heart and lungs to convert oxygen into energy for the muscles. Exercise which increases your heartbeat and breathing rate for a sustained period is aerobic or cardiovascular exercise. The difference you notice when you have done some cardiovascular exercise over a period of time is that you are *less* out of breath walking or running up a flight of stairs, or running for a bus, or while joining in a sport. You can do more before your system starts to feel stressed. Building well on your cardiovascular fitness gives great feelings of buoyancy and positivity which spread through all the other aspects of your life.

Why do we get into problems with cardiovascular fitness, and why might we need to take positive steps to improve it? There is far less inevitable cardiovascular activity in everyday life than there was in our parents' or grandparents' generations. Where our parents might have walked to local shops daily and carried moderately heavy bags of shopping home, thus having a little cardiovascular and a little toning exercise, we would tend to travel to a supermarket by car, buy a week's provisions, and load it into the car to drive home again. Laundry and ironing were immensely physically demanding chores only a generation or two ago, with loading and unloading and manoeuvring bulky twin-tub machines (or earlier still, heavy coppers), stretching up and down to washing lines, and hand rinsing, scrubbing and wringing, working the body hard cardiovascularly as well as maintaining flexibility in the joints. Even gardening – still a way of getting up a good sweat fairly easily – was far harder work when mowers and rollers had to be pushed rather than being motor-driven.

I have no desire to cast a spurious sentimental glow over the labour-intensive way ordinary life-maintaining chores used to be. For many people all that that meant was restriction and exhaustion, far from glowing health. Furthermore, if one's job or one's life involved doing particular heavy chores repeatedly, one's body was bound to develop unevenly. It is a first-world affluent privilege to be able to choose to develop our bodies evenly and thoughtfully all over. We do need to notice, however, that owning machines which do many of those chores with minimal physical effort is not pure gain. We pay a triple price of losing an occasion for vigorous physical activity, potentially feeling rather alien and remote from the nitty gritty of life (think of the profound affection some people do have for extremely messy and tiring tasks like taking cars apart and putting them together again, or organizing attics or cupboards, or having major gardening sessions), and, by using more energy and pollutants, compromising the atmosphere in which we move. That final part may sound a bit far-reaching or stressfully political/philosophical when all we are reviewing at the moment is how our heart and lungs work and how to improve them; but once you begin to care about how your body feels and how it is working, it is only a small step to start being interested in how the elements around you are faring. Particularly when the issue is cardiovascular fitness, you become increasingly aware of how the universe moves into and out of you in the form of the gases that are taken in and exchanged in your lungs. This focuses the mind very clearly on the quality of those gases, and on the interactivity between the materials in the universe and the materials which make up you. Once you care about that, you care about the state of the planet as well.

Since we rely more and more on machinery to do heavy labour, and cars to make even the shortest journey, our cardiovascular fitness can easily run right down. Our aim in Project One, then, is to begin to build that cardiovascular fitness up again. For some people this is the easiest part of becoming fit for the first time, or of becoming fit again after a period of inactivity. Many people find it far easier to take up walking, running, cycling, or rowing than they do to work on their flexibility or adjust their eating habits. Their cardiovascular improvement graph is rapid and satisfying. Others, and I am one of them, find this the most daunting part of their fitness programme. I have both a history of asthma and a history of being a younger sister always scrambling unsuccessfully to keep up with the older kids! Thus I grew up believing I could not run, so I ran less and less, so I became less and less able to run and very inhibited about taking part in sport of any kind. It is only since I grew up and became fit via oriental disciplines (yoga, martial arts), where the focus is on the struggle within, as opposed to occidental sports where the focus is on competition with others, that I have been able to run at all.

So, if you approach cardiovascular training with a sinking heart, you are not alone. Think over any events or patterns in your life which might have made you feel tense or inadequate about the sort of exercise that challenges and develops your heart and lungs. Then remind yourself that you do not have to tackle this by throwing on revealing shorts and expensive running shoes and making an exhibition of yourself in the street. You can start instead very gradually, and remain very private about it for as long as you want to.

Step by step

To improve gradually you need to begin by working out what your training zone is, and getting yourself into that training zone for short periods several times a week, then increasing and sustaining the training periods for longer.

Subtract your age from 220: this gives you your maximum heart rate. Aim to train at 70–80% of this number. For instance, for a 30-year-old, the maximum heart rate is 190 (220 minus 30) and the training rate is between 133 (70% of 190) and 162 (80% of 190) heart-beats per minute.

Walking

Look at your cardiovascular requirement in Week One. It is simply to walk for 10 minutes, 3 times during that week, briskly enough to bring your pulse up to your training rate. You will feel rather warm at the time, and rather pleasant afterwards (due to the release of endorphins into your bloodstream), but you should not feel any stress at all. Walk with your back long, your shoulders relaxed, and your hips mobile. Tick off the three boxes, one after each walk, and make a note in the comments box. It might be something like:

'I had forgotten how nice it was to walk through the autumn leaves.'

or

'It made me think about the kind of shoes I wear.'

just as much as,

'My left knee is a bit stiff, but loosening up with the walking.'

or,

'Ten minutes isn't so very long to walk briskly. Perhaps I can manage it.'

The second Week is the same although you should find any residual breathlessness is easing by now.

The next step

In Week Three you should do two 10-minute brisk walks and then begin to think about what you would like to choose as your secondary cardiovascular training activity. You might like to begin some jogging, you might like to ride a push-bike or a stationary bike, or use a rowing machine, or skip with a skipping rope. Choose whichever of those you feel drawn to, and do up to

5 minutes of that as well. If you want to jog and it is very hard, try walking 50 steps then running 50 steps, gradually working up to 75/75, 100/100, and so on until you can jog continuously for 5 minutes. Do not allow yourself to gasp for breath. Work only to your own comfortable maximum within your training rate. Use the same slow build-up technique with skipping, rowing, or cycling if you need to. At the end of each session tick the boxes. At the end of the week, record your comment.

Week Four is the same as Week Three, except that you will begin to feel more comfortable with the second string to your cardiosvascular bow.

In Week Five you swop around to having two 5-minute sessions on the second activity (jogging, skipping, etc.) and one 10-minute walk. Then, reading off your chart, you can see you develop 3 second activities up to three 10-minute sessions each per week, and begin to look around for a class or a sport you would like to participate in which has a significant cardiovascular element. Take your time over this: just see if there is something you feel attracted to. Do not do anything about it yet unless you are quite sure you feel ready.

Flexibility

Flexibility is the element in any training package that I find easy. Twenty years of yoga have opened up my physical flexibility tremendously, so stretching holds no fears for me, only interest at new ideas or positions. Many of my male colleagues, however, protest that they find it far 'easier' to go for a run than to settle down to even ten or fifteen minutes' work on flexibility. It is true that because of the effect of different hormone balances on the joints and ligaments, men do have a slightly harder time becoming flexible in the first place, but it really is only a small difference. What puts men (and women) off about stretching is the 'I-can't-do-it-so-I-don't-do-it-so-I-can't-do-it' cycle which affects me about cardiovascular fitness. So, we can break out of that cycle by beginning to stretch.

Basic stretching

Your stretching task for Week One is to pick a time of day when you can do some stretching, and learn the basic set. A basic set includes a forward bend, a back bend, a sideways bend, a leg stretch, and a twist. Starting off like that we are just oiling the joints. Later on we can move on to further variations and the body will open out like a flower. Move into and out of every stretch slowly and carefully.

BASIC FORWARD BEND

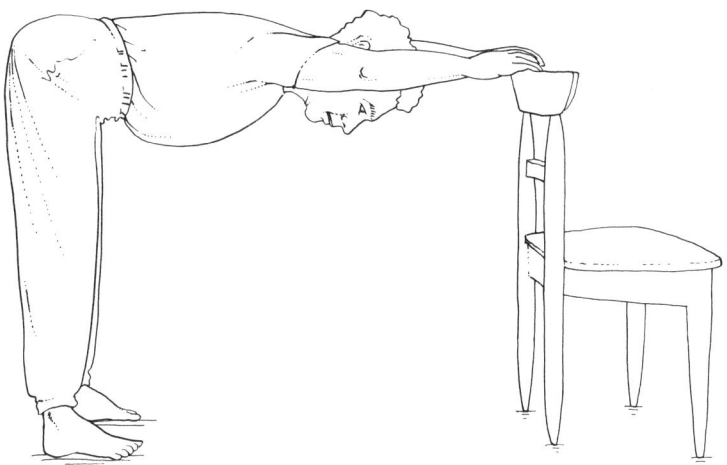

- Stand with your feet hip-distance apart and centre your weight equally between left foot and right, ball of the foot and heel. Relax your shoulders and your face. Breathe in and stretch up out of your hips. Exhaling, stretch into a forward bend. Hold on to a table or the back of a chair. Remember, the hinge you bend at is at the top of your thigh bone, not in the back of your waist, or up in between your shoulder blades. Keep your back as flat as you can, and think of the spine being a groove rather than a row of humps. At your comfortable maximum, relax your head and neck. You should feel a sensation of stretching up the backs of your legs, and in the back and arms. Never, never bounce in a stretch, increase the stretch with your breath and think of it as the body opening up. When you are ready to come up (10 seconds is plenty to start with), inhale and lift your head, exhale and *walk towards the support* to come up. Never, never fling yourself up from this forward bend, or you will hurt your lower back. Always walk towards your support to come up.

BASIC BACK BEND

As children we all enjoyed arching and stretching our spines backwards, scuttling along in 'crab' position, and lying on our tummies, pulling our feet back into a 'bow' or 'rocking horse' pose. All too often this range of movement gets lost in our adult lives, as life in a busy home and/or workplace rarely provides us with any opportunities to get into such positions! If you have not pushed up from the floor into a 'bridge' or 'crab' position since you were eight years old, do not suddenly get down and attempt it at 38 years or it will have dire consequences. Begin with this very gentle back bend.

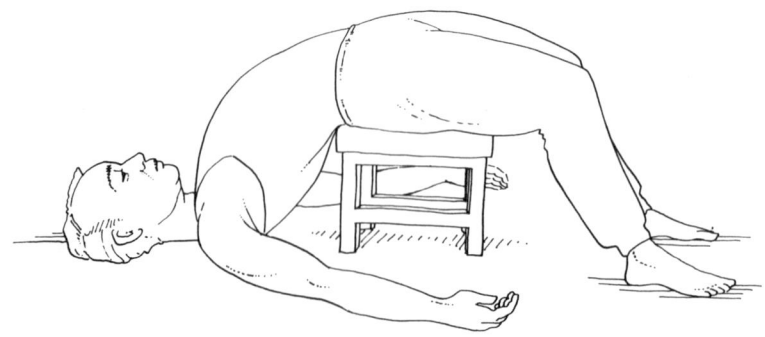

- Lie flat on your back, with your knees bent, your feet parallel, hip distance apart and flat on the ground, close to your buttocks. Relax your back into the ground, ease your shoulders down a little towards your waist, ease your neck along the ground away from your shoulders.

- Inhaling, take your thoughts down into your feet, spread your toes and heels into the ground. Exhaling, stretch your knees away from you, lengthen in the thighs, and gently lift the hips and lower spine off the floor. Either relax the arms and hands (palms upwards) alongside you on the floor, or support your back with your hands. It is very relaxing to lift up into this stretch over a low stool (see illustration). Breathe steadily and relax your face and throat. Your chest will feel beautifully open and free and your spine pleasantly stretched.

- When you are ready to come down (10 seconds is plenty to start with), do so on an exhalation with a feeling of making your spine long as you come down to the floor. Then slowly hug your knees onto your chest and feel your lower back spread warmly into the ground.

BASIC SIDE STRETCH

- Stand with your feet 3 to 3½ feet apart, left foot turned in, right foot turned out. Inhale and stretch your arms straight out to the side, at shoulder level. Exhale and relax your shoulders, lengthen your arms, stretching right into the fingertips. Breathe in again, and on the breath out stretch out to the right and then down, resting your right hand on thigh, knee, foot, or floor, whatever is right for you today.
- Do not bounce or force it. Only go as far as is creating a stretch, but not a strain.
- Keep your hips and your chest facing the front. Turn and look at the upper thumb with the lower eye. Breathe steadily and hold the stretch – 10 seconds is plenty of time to hold at first.
- When you want to come up, feel the left foot is firm on the floor and the left leg is strong. Breathe in and come up, arms at shoulder level. Exhale and slowly lower your arms to your sides.
- Repeat the stretch, with equal focus and attention, to the other side. You feel an opening and mobilizing throughout the body in this side stretch.

BASIC LEG STRETCH

There are thousands of different ways of opening up and stretching legs and hips. We will use this one to start with because it has so many benefits, working on hips, groin, inner thighs and knees.

- Sit tall, coming right up out of your hips. Lift your abdomen, relax your shoulders. Bring the soles of your feet together and draw them in as close to you as possible. Release your knees down towards the floor. Do not bounce your knees up and down. Check once more that you are sitting well up, then hold the stretch and breathe, for 10 seconds or so. Come out of the stretch by gently lifting your knees up with your hands, and then stretching your legs straight out in front of you.

- If you are tired, or it is difficult to keep your spine upright, do this stretch supported by a wall. Do not think about forcing your knees to the floor. Think of opening up and letting tightness go. One day, you will look down and see to your astonishment your knees *are* on the floor.

BASIC TWIST

In twisting stretches we begin to move the upper axis of the body, the shoulders, in the opposite direction to the lower axis, the hips. Eventually, all sorts of interesting lengthenings and strengthenings take place. Let us begin with a basic twist.

- Sitting on the floor, stretch your right leg straight out in front of you, bend your left knee, and put the foot flat on the floor, close to the perineum.

- Put your left hand on the floor behind you and, leaning gently back onto it, turn to your left, putting your right armpit to the left of your left knee. Exhaling, straighten your spine up, centre your weight in your hips, turn and look over your left shoulder, and turn your right palm to face outwards. Breathe steadily in the stretch, face and throat soft, and remain for up to 10 seconds to start with.

- When you are ready, on an exhalation, untangle yourself, and then repeat the stretch, for the same length of time, and with the same attention and focus, on the other side.

LIE DOWN

- Finally, lie on the floor on your back. Stretch out in a 'starfish' shape – arms and legs stretching away from the body at an angle. Think of it as an all-over yawn, and repeat two or three times, then settle down lying with your feet flopped slightly apart and your arms rolled a little way away from your sides. Rest and relax for 2 or 3 minutes before moving on to the next part of your day.

Look at your Week One chart. You will see that your requirement is to set aside three 10-minute periods to learn the basic stretching. You can do these after cardiovascular work if you like, or separately if that is more convenient. Tick off the sessions in the boxes as you do them.

In Weeks Two, Three and Four do the basic stretching as before, slowly and thoughtfully. By Week Four, aim to be holding the stretches for 20 seconds each. Do not forget to write your comments down too.

In Weeks Five and Six do the basic stretching and also learn these variations, one per session.

VARIATION ONE: FORWARD BEND

- Stand with your feet 3 to 3½ feet apart and turn your left foot in, your right foot out. Put your hands on your hips, and, on an exhalation, turn to face over your right leg. Turn your chest and hips in the direction of your right toes, and try to line up your sternum (breastbone) into the same line as your knee.
- Breathe in, and lift up out of your hips. Exhaling, stretch forwards, back as flat as you can, torso parallel with the floor. The crown of your head extends away, your neck and face are relaxed. Breathe steadily and remain in the stretch for up to 10 seconds, then inhale and lift your head, exhale, feel your feet and legs are strong, and come up.
- Repeat the stretch in the other direction.
- You can also do this stretch reaching your arms out in front of you and holding onto a table or a heavy chair. As you loosen up you can gradually stretch down along the forward leg.

VARIATION TWO: SIDE STRETCH

- Stand your feet 4 to 4½ feet apart, and turn the left foot in, the right foot out. Inhaling, bring your arms up to shoulder level, exhaling, relax the shoulders, stretch the arms, *and* bend the right knee so that the thigh is parallel to the floor, the shin vertical. Breathe in again, and, as you exhale, stretch out to the right (elongate the right side of your waist) and then rest your right elbow on your right knee. Take the left arm up and over, giving a wonderful stretch along the whole of the left side of the body.
- Breathe steadily, with your face and throat relaxed. This is a powerful stretch and 5 seconds may be quite enough at first. When you are ready, visualize your legs and feet as firm and strong, then breathe in to come up.

- Now do the stretch to the other side, this time giving the right side of your body that wonderful stretch.

VARIATION THREE: LEG STRETCH

- Sit tall, with your legs straight out in front of you. Lift your buttocks out to the sides (yes, go on!) to make sure you are sitting in the centre of your pelvic floor. Inhaling, lift up out of your hips, and exhaling stretch forwards, remembering again that the hinge is at the top of your thighs, not the back of your waist or in between your shoulder blades. If your feet seem miles away, hook a belt or a scarf around them and hold onto it in order to pull yourself forwards keeping your back flat. Think of travelling forwards rather than down. Do not bounce or strain, simply feel a stretch. Eventually you will lie down along the tops of your legs: on day one this seems impossible, and on day 31 it seems impossible too, but somewhere between then and day 101, it simply happens. The strong and pleasurable stretch is felt along the backs of the legs.

VARIATION FOUR: TWIST

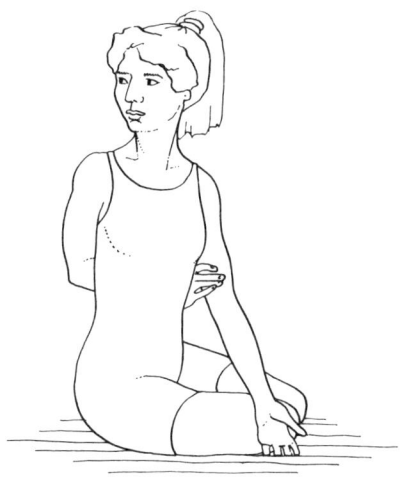

- For this twist, sit up tall, and tuck your right heel into your perineum, and your left heel right round behind you. If this feels very difficult, put one or two cushions or pillows underneath your hips and try again. Sit up tall, relax your shoulders, and lift your abdomen. Place the back of your left hand against the top of your right knee. Breathe in. As you exhale, turn to look over your right shoulder, and place your right hand on the floor behind you. Keep your weight in your hips – do not let it all fall back onto your right hand. Visualize your spine as a spiral staircase, the twist beginning at the base of it and moving evenly up. Breathe steadily, and keep your face and throat soft.
- When you are ready, exhaling, release your stretch, and then repeat it in the other direction, with the same attention and for the same length of time.

In Weeks Seven, Eight, Nine and Ten, increase the stretching time to three 15-minute sessions. Incorporate all four variations into your session in the appropriate sequence; i.e. do the basic forward bend, then forward bend variation, the basic side bend, then the side bend variation, and so forth.

Gradually increase the length of time you spend in each stretch to 25 to 30 seconds, but never, never force the strain. Stretching time is a time for thoughtful and loving exploration of your body and how it feels.

During Week Eleven, do your stretches as above, and learn one more stretch.

VARIATION FIVE: BACK BEND

- After ten weeks of this stretching programme, your spine will be awakening and mobilizing. Start to work on a new back bend. Lie on the floor on your tummy, palms on the floor, close to your sides at shoulder level. Turn your face to the floor, breathe in. As you exhale, lift your upper body up off the floor, keeping your pubic bone and legs on the floor. Relax your shoulders; do not let them hunch up into your ears. You may only come up a few inches – that is fine, do not strain, just come up to the right place for you. As soon as you have had enough – five seconds may be plenty at first – flow forwards down onto the floor, rest your face to one side and your arms alongside your body. When you are ready, repeat this stretch once more, then push up onto all fours, and on an exhalation stretch your bottom back towards your heels, and stretch your arms out in front of you. This pleasant counter-stretch evens out the sensations in the back, and is known as 'praying stretch'.

When you do this back bend, always try to rise up off the floor with body strength rather than hand and arm strength; i.e. do not push down hard into your hands as a primary method of lifting up.

Gradually increase the amount of time you spend in this back bend, always remembering to follow it with the counter-stretch.

In Week Twelve do all the stretches you have learned. Spend up to 30 seconds in each stretch. Look back over your progress during those 12 weeks and allow yourself to feel the pleasure of progress and rediscovery in your flexibility.

Toning

The goal of muscle-toning exercises is to strengthen and define our muscular tone evenly all over. We often have strong arms from everyday lifting, or strong legs from, say, cycling or walking, but weak abdominals, or under-developed pectorals, or undefined trapezius and latissimus dorsi (the muscles on the back), or flabby gluteal muscles (the bottom!). Never mind. As we said earlier, the good news starts here; we are about to start to do something about it, and we are starting by celebrating where we are now, as well as celebrating where we hope to be in a few months' time.

Where developing the cardiovascular system gives a sense of strength, endurance and buoyancy, and developing flexibility gives fluency and a sense of deeper insight in the body, toning gives a sense of pleasant tightness and lightness. It also promotes a feeling of articulation, of the whole body hanging together properly. If you are very unevenly toned, as most of us are before we do any particular work on it, what happens is that the stronger areas of the body take over some of the work that should be done by the weaker parts. For example, in those of us who have weak abdominals, the spine is being supported chiefly by the muscles around the back. They cope with a lot of additional strain because of this and may ache. The curve at the back of the spine may be more pronounced than is ideal, further stressing the abdominal muscles by spilling all the contents of the pelvis forwards onto them.

After a few weeks of working on toning the abdominal muscles there is a pronounced change. Because these muscles are stronger, you recognize the sensation that they are doing most of the work of supporting the spine: that it is held up from in front as well as from behind. This is the beginning of the enjoyable sensation of 'everything pulling together'.

Look at your Week One chart for toning. The required activity in Week One is that you set aside 10 minutes, three times during the week, to learn the basic toning exercise. In your first session, learn the upper body and arm exercises; in the second, the abdominal exercises; in the third, the hip and leg exercises. During Weeks Two, Three and Four, simply repeat them, at 10 repetitions (reps) each, concentrating on 'correct form' – that is, on keeping each exercise neat, tidy and controlled, and avoiding doing it by throwing yourself around.

Be realistic. If 3 or 4 reps of a particular exercise is all you can do at first, that is fine; 3 or 4 good accurate reps is a good beginning. Before long you will be able to add a couple more, and then a couple more, until you are up to the basic 10.

Basic toning

Always begin your toning exercises with a short warm-up, unless you are doing them after your flexibility exercises, in which case you are already nice and loose.

SHORT WARM-UP

1 Stand tall with your feet hip-distance apart, tailbone tucked in, abdomen lifted, shoulders relaxed. Drop your chin onto your chest, then slowly sweep it up towards your right shoulder. Sweep back down to the centre, then slowly up to the left. Do this 4 or 5 times until your neck starts to feel more relaxed, then slowly rotate the head, a few times in one direction and a few times in the other. Finish with your chin on your chest in the centre, then exhaling, float it up.

2 Rotate your shoulders in big, slow circles, 6 times forward, and 6 times backwards.

3 Put your hands on your hips and relax your knees a little. Make big, slow circles with your hips in a movement like belly dancing. Go 6 times in one direction, and 6 times in the other.

4 If it is easy for you to get into a squatting position, do so. Bring your heels to the floor if you can. Ease your elbows in between your knees and place your palms together, opening the inner thighs. Lift your spine as much as you can.

   Then, place your right hand on the floor and stretch your left leg out straight, hold for a few seconds, then change.

   Stand up, shake your arms and legs, and you are ready to start.

   If squatting is not yet comfortable for you, get into a squatting position on a low stool or on the edge of an ordinary chair to achieve the same effect. As you become more limber, you will eventually be able to squat easily.

ARMS AND UPPER BODY

1 Stand with your feet hip-distance apart. Tuck your tail bone in, lift your abdomen and relax your shoulders. Exhaling, stretch your arms out at shoulder level. On your next exhalation, bend your elbows. Have your hands in loose fists, your forearms up vertical, upper arms out horizontal. Now bring your forearms together in front of your face, then stretch them out to the side again. Repeat rhythmically and with attention, for 10 reps. Keep your shoulders down away from your ears, and breathe steadily.

2 Use the same stance: feet hip-distance apart, abdomen lifting, shoulders relaxed. Have your arms in by your sides and, exhaling, make loose fists with your hands. Bend your elbows, so your fists face in to your armpits. Now straighten your arms out behind you as high as you can without straining. At the maximum stretch open your hands; palms down to the floor. Repeat briskly and with attention for 10 reps.

3 Wall push ups. Stand one to one-and-a-half feet away from the wall, place your hands flat on the wall, fingers facing in towards each other. Exhaling, straighten your arms to push up, inhaling, bend your elbows to come in close to the wall. Keep your body straight, and your arms and chest will do the

work. Moving at the natural speed of your own breath, do 10 reps. Now circle your shoulders a few times forwards, a few times backwards, easing any tension in the arms and neck.

ABDOMINALS

1. Lie on your back, knees bent, feet flat on the floor and hip-distance apart. Put both hands on your lower abdomen. Exhaling, press the back of your waist into the floor and smoothly roll your pubic bone upwards, as though you were aiming it towards your navel. Inhaling, release, exhaling roll. Go on for 10 reps. With your hands on your lower abdominal muscles, you will begin to feel those muscles working, and that is the first stage of becoming reacquainted with these elusive muscles!

By the way, almost all women, and many men, get very upset when they put their hands on their soft abdomens. Try not to hate your body. In my experience, work done *with* your body in loving alliance is a lot more productive in the long run than work done *on* the body as though it were a delinquent client of some sort.

2. Stay in the same position, but move one hand to the area above the navel, and keep the other on the area below the navel. Press the back of the waist into the ground, then, exhaling, press the whole abdomen back towards the spine. Inhaling, relax. Repeat, in the rhythm of your own breathing, for 10 reps. This also gives you a feeling of how your abdominal muscles work.

3. Keep your hands as they are and stay in the same position on the floor. Press the back of your waist into the floor. Let your chin move outwards a bit as though you were trying to hold an apple underneath it, then, exhaling, lift your head a couple of inches off the floor, inhaling, return to the floor. Repeat 10 times. Be very aware of how your abdominals are working, and be aware of keeping them pressed back towards the spine as you lift up.

It is well worth spending your abdominal toning time on these basics at first. You may be desperate to flatten your abdomen and longing to get cracking with sequences of crunches and sit-ups, but until you get a real feeling of *how* to do those things so that it is your abdomen and not your back doing the work, you will waste a lot of endeavour. So bear with these foundation exercises for the first two weeks.

HIPS

1   Again, lie on your back, knees bent and feet flat on the floor, and lay your arms by your sides, rolled a little way away from your sides, palms upwards.
    Exhaling, squeeze your bottom tight, and, inhaling, release. You will feel activity in your bottom and thighs. Squeeze and release in the rhythm of your own breathing, 10 times.

2   Staying in the same position, exhaling, squeeze the muscles in your bottom, and then, keeping it all squeezed, lift your bottom up into the air. Keep your pubic bone rolling up as if you were tipping it towards your navel. Inhaling, let your hips down almost, but not quite, to the floor. Exhaling, lift up again, inhaling lower, and continue in the rhythm of your own breathing for 10 repetitions. If 10 is too many at first, just do what you can. When I first learned this exercise I could do 4! Just start from where you are, and build from there.

Pelvic floor exercises are good for women and for men. The pelvic floor is the area which would be covered by a sanitary towel, if you were wearing one, or, alternatively, the bit of you which would be in contact with a bicycle saddle if you were riding a bike.

Given that we stand upright instead of going round on all fours, our pelvic floors, particularly clearly for women, are holding our insides in, so should be attended to and kept nice and springy.

It is also clear that keeping the anal sphincter muscle active and responsive improves general comfort and relaxation about bowel movements. For women, improving tone in the vaginal muscles certainly improves sexual response. Most women know that pelvic floor exercises improve their sexual response by making it easier to have an orgasm, but I want to share the news that just as crucial to sexual enjoyment for women is being able to control the *angle* of *entry* and that this can be achieved by both the hip and pelvic floor exercise, together increasing finesse in the whole area!

Pelvic floor exercises improve circulation to the perineum and as such are a good way of helping the health of the prostate. Finally, urinary incontinence in both sexes is kept at bay by regular pelvic floor exercise.

3 With all these things in mind, then, do some pelvic floor squeezes every day. Tighten up the pelvic floor area as if you were trying not to go to the loo. Relax. Squeeze and release 10 times, finishing with a gentle squeeze. Tie this exercise into something you do regularly, like boiling a kettle, or stopping at red traffic lights, or standing over a fax machine. At first it is quite hard to 'contact' the muscles, but gradually you will get very adept at it.

LEGS

1 Pile up a couple of phone books, or 2 or 3 thick dictionaries against the skirting board. Make sure they will not skid apart; or, if you have an exercise step, use that. Stand tall, with your toes on the step and your heels hanging over the edge of it. Your abdomen is lifting, your shoulders relaxed, and you are keeping your balance with your fingertips against the wall. Exhaling, smoothly come up onto tiptoes, inhaling drop your heels smoothly down again. In the rhythm of your own breathing, continue to come up and down, feeling the work in your calves. Do 10 reps.

2 Lie on your left side, legs stretched out straight and hips stacked vertically one over the other. Support your upper body on your left forearm to your left and your right palm in front of you. Keep a big distance between your shoulders and your ears.

Exhaling, lift the top leg up, with control, and, inhaling, bring it down to the lower leg again. Aim for 10 reps with control; resist the temptation to swing your leg up and down – move it deliberately and smoothly. Exhale on the way up, inhale on the way down.

Now change sides: lie on your right side and aim for 10 reps on this side, with just as much control. You may find you are startlingly asymmetrical; not to worry, do your best, and you will even up in time. Next time, start on your more difficult side so that your best energy goes into that side, and you will even up more quickly. You will feel work in the inner and outer thighs.

3 Come onto all fours, with your knees hip-distance apart, your hands shoulder-distance apart. Breathing in, curve your back like a cat, drop your head, and bring your right knee in towards your nose. Exhaling, lift your head and, at the same time, straighten your right leg out behind you and then up as far as you comfortably can. Repeat the movement smoothly and with control, 4 more times on this side, then 5 times on the left. Finish by sitting back on your heels and stretching your hands and arms out on the floor in front of you. You will feel the work on the fronts of your thighs, and it is pleasant to finish in this stretch.

During Weeks One and Two, become familiar with these exercises, and try and get them all up to 10 reps. During Weeks Three to Six, take the same exercises up to 20 reps each, step by step with a few reps increase every day apart from the pelvic floor exercise, which you should continue to do in sets of 10 on and off during the day at the trigger points you have decided on. The only change in exercise is in the abdominal section which from Week Three onwards becomes as follows.

Further abdominals

By now you are beginning to have a sense of how and when your abdominal muscles work. Whenever you learn a new abdominal exercise, check it out with a hand (either your own or someone else's if the exercise does not leave you with one free!) on the relevant bit of your abdomen to see that it is working the way you want it to. Particularly, be careful to flex your abdomen back towards your spine as you exercise it, or you may develop muscles which, although their tone is good, protrude.

Now that you know your way round your abdomen, learn the following exercises.

1   Lie on your back with your knees bent, feet flat on the floor, and the back of your waist pressed gently towards the floor, pubic bone curved up towards your navel. Clasp your hands behind your head, elbows well out to the sides. Flatten the abdomen into the spine, move your chin out as though you were holding an apple under it, and, exhaling, sit up so that your shoulders and head come off the ground. Inhaling go back down. Continue up and down for 10 reps. If it feels like very hard work, clasp your knees onto your chest as you finish, and breathe deeply.

2   Go back to the original position, this time with your right hand behind your head, and your left arm straight out alongside you, palm facing the ceiling. Cross your left foot onto your right thigh and let your left knee fall out to the side. Flatten your abdomen and, exhaling, bring your right elbow towards your left knee (it does not have to touch it). Inhaling go back down. Continue in the rhythm of your own breathing for 10 reps. Now change positions and do 10 on the other side.

3   Start in the original position as for exercise 1 in this group. Stretch your arms out to the sides at shoulder level. As you exhale, turn and look at your left hand, and let your knees go down to the ground on the right. Remain there for 5 breaths, then, inhaling, come back to the centre, exhaling look to the right and drop your knees to the left. Remain for 5 breaths before coming back to the centre and finishing.

For Weeks Seven to Twelve, push the reps up to 30 per exercise except for the Further Abdominals, which you should take up to 15, or, if 15 begins to get too easy, get it up to 20; and for the pelvic floor exercises, which you should continue to do in sets of 10 during the day at the trigger points you have decided on for yourself.

Stress management and relaxation

We know that stress is the modern professionals' epidemic, being potentially in the whole range of possible activities from overload to redundancy. Doing the physical elements of the Project will, without a doubt, lower your stress levels, because you will be rebalancing the imbalance which exists for so many urban professionals between physical and intellectual work. Even so, it is worth developing some skills and insights into specific stress management and relaxation techniques. As with the other elements of our projects, let us start with the simple and achievable, and get confident and complicated later.

Abdominal breathing

Your Weeks One, Two and Three charts show that you should take three 5-minute sessions to learn and then become familiar with practising abdominal breathing. You may well want to do these sessions after one of your other 10-minute spots. Play around with combinations of the four different disciplines you are learning (cardiovascular, flexibility, toning, relaxation). You may want to stack them together as three 40-minute workouts per week, or it may be more sensible for you to interleave them between the other bits of your life in 5- and 10-minute sections. Find out what suits you.

Why breathing? Well, breathing is strongly linked with emotional and spiritual expression. How do you breathe when you are scared? What about when you are bored? How do you breathe when you are making love? How do you breathe when you are tense and impatient? You can probably feel easily what those different kinds of breathing would be like.

Now imagine how you breathe when you are very peaceful. We are going to learn to breathe that way even when we are *not*

36 Fit To Work

peaceful, because doing so will help us to relocate that feeling of peace when we need it.

- Sit in a chair with your hips well back, your spine supported on the chair back, your legs uncrossed and feet flat on the floor. Relax your shoulders and lift the crown of your head. Draw your chin in slightly so that the back of your neck is long.

Read the remaining instructions and either become familiar with them or tape them, with appropriate pauses, for yourself to listen to while you get used to them.

- Place your right hand on your abdomen below your navel, and your left hand, palm up, on your left knee or the arm of the chair. Let your eyes close. Start to breathe a little bit more deeply, a little bit more slowly than usual. Hear the breath as it comes and goes. When you have settled into a rhythm, start to breathe in through your nose, and out through your mouth. Do not blow the breath out, simply part your lips and let the air escape.

- When you are breathing easily in through the nose and out through the mouth, start to become aware of your hand on your abdomen. As you breathe in, send the breath all the way down to that hand. Feel the abdomen swell slightly into it. As you breathe out, let the breath come back up from behind the hand.

- Feel the abdomen collapse back from it slightly. Breathing in, you fill up, the abdomen pushes into your hand. Breathing out, you empty, and the abdomen falls back from the hand. Continue in your own rhythm. This is not an exaggerated puffing in and out. It is a small movement.

- Now do one last thing. Make a tiny pause between each breath. Breathe in, and hesitate; breathe out, and hesitate. Continue in your own rhythm.

- Carry on for as long as feels right for you. Remind yourself from time to time to sit up tall. You will come to a natural point where you want to stop: you might get bored, or other thoughts might start to cross your mind. That is fine.

- When you are ready to stop, take your hand away from your abdomen, and rest it on your knee or the arm of your chair. Let your breathing return to an everyday level. Blink your eyes open and slowly let in the light.
- Do not rush around. Pause for a moment to enjoy the peace you have generated, simply by controlling your breathing, before moving into the next part of your day.

Savasana – deep relaxation

On the chart for Weeks Four, Five, and Six in the relaxation section, you can see 5 minutes set aside three times a week to begin to get to know *savasana* – deep relaxation. As with abdominal breathing, you may want to do this at the end of one or more of your other sections. Wrap up warmly before you do *savasana* or you will get chilled – add an extra sweatshirt and some socks.

- Lie down on the floor on your back. If you have any tension in your lower back, hug your knees towards your chest for a little while, then straighten your legs.

Read these instructions through until you are familiar with them, or, if it is more convenient for you to do so, read them onto tape and play them until you have assimilated them all.

- Start by taking your awareness to your feet. Breathing in, tighten your feet a little, exhaling, relax them. Let your feet roll naturally apart a little. Feel that they are heavy on the ground. Now take your awareness to your legs: your thighs, your knees, and your calves. Breathing in, tighten up your legs a little, and, exhaling, relax them, let them go. Feel your legs warm and heavy on the ground.
- Tighten up your buttock muscles, pull your abdomen in towards your spine, then release and relax your hips – feel them heavy on the ground. Feel your lower back spreading out, and the back of your waist spreading out.

- Make gentle fists with your hands, lift your arms an inch or two off the ground, and tighten your arm muscles. Exhaling, relax from upper arms to fingertips, let your arms rest on the floor, rolled naturally out a little way from your sides; feel your arms and hands warm and heavy.

- If you feel you would like to, shift your shoulder blades down towards your waist a little. Take a deep breath in, fill your lungs up to the collar bones. Breathe it out with a sigh, and then let your breath come and go as it wants to. It will probably take on a light, even rhythm.

- If your lips feel dry, moisten them with your tongue, and then let your tongue rest in your mouth below the lower set of teeth.

- Squeeze your eyes more tightly shut and grimace with your whole face, then let your face relax and be smooth and soft. Feel your head heavy on the ground.

- You will not fall through the floor, the floor will hold you however relaxed you become. Relax a little more, let the floor do it all.

When you first do this, it may put you to sleep completely, so arrange some kind of mechanism for being woken up if, for instance, you decide to do it in your office in the lunch hour but do not especially want to be found prone on the floor by your two o'clock appointment! The aim eventually is to be very peaceful but still awake.

Spend the natural amount of time for you in *savasana* – it will probably be 5 minutes or so at first – and you will begin to have an impulse to wake yourself up. Do this by spending as much time as you need yawning and stretching all over. When you want to get up, do so by curling up and rolling over onto your side first, then pushing your hands into the floor to help yourself up. Do not rush around; spend a few moments experiencing the sense of peace you have created simply by relaxing.

Look on the charts for Weeks Seven to Twelve. You will see that there are now three 10-minute stress management sections.

In your 10 minutes, do 5 minutes' abdominal breathing, followed by 5 minutes' *savasana*. Add this 10 minutes onto the end of another part of the programme if you like, or do it separately if that works better for you. Do not forget to note down your comments as the weeks go on and you become more adept at accessing your inner peace.

Lifestyle

The lifestyle section of the Project is the most difficult to define in some ways, but although it is elusive, it is just as important as the very specific skills of exercise and relaxation which we are developing.

It is concerned with stopping the splitting between self and health, self and fitness, self and body-image, and self and self-esteem that we are very inclined to fall into in the West.

'I have poor self-esteem', we say, as though 'poor self-esteem' was a car that we owned, or, 'I have health problems', as though 'health problems' was some kind of machine which did not work properly. We *are* our self-esteem, we *are* our state of health, and the sooner we realize that, the sooner we can reintegrate all the different bits of ourselves into a fit and healthy whole. In English we have a linguistic predisposition to this kind of splitting: where in English we say 'I have a cold' or 'I have cancer', many other European languages say the equivalent of 'I am colding' or 'I am cancering'.

In the lifestyle section of Project One, we are looking at raising our awareness of how we eat, how we use caffeine, alcohol and nicotine, and how we perceive ourselves. We are going to do this in a fresh and open-hearted way. Many of us already have extensive experience of 'policing' our food and eating, and know just how counter-productive the totalitarian food-police state is. On any one day, 25 per cent of women in the UK are on diets, with 50 per cent finishing, breaking or starting one. At the very least, this is a major distraction factor which stops many women from achieving their full professional potential because they are worrying about food. Certainly the women in modern Western culture who are genuinely overweight are more likely to be so because of eating disturbances caused by on-and-off dieting since adolescence than for any other reason. The weight-loss cult has a fatal margin – 150,000 young women die of anorexia in America every year (which is more than the number of fatalities in ten years of civil war in Beirut).

Police-style dieting has a huge impact on every female person growing up in the affluent West. Whether they take part in it or not, they are aware of it all around them, all the time. Its effects on men are not yet documented and quantified, and far less pervasive, since 'achieving' a low body-weight is a far less pressing cultural imperative for men (who are much more likely to be harassed about sexual 'score' and performance, and frank muscular strength). The hideous irony is that, while young women die of anorexia in the UK and USA, the rest of the population of the world is frantically trying to get enough to eat, and often not succeeding.

All we want to do then, for now, is to begin to take notice of what we eat, when, and how it makes us feel. Take time every day for Weeks One to Four to notice what kinds of food you ate and how you felt: how was your skin, your hair, your gut, your moods, your emotions? What did you most enjoy? If you have been on and off many diets, all sorts of tangled emotions may arise. Write them down. If there is not enough room in the boxes, paper-clip extra paper in to record your thoughts. If you are anorexic or bulimic now, *please* acknowledge it, first to yourself, then to a person or organization you trust to enable you to move away from these life-threatening conditions. On this part of the Project we are not making any evaluations whatsoever; we are simply starting to do some noticing.

Use the lifestyle space on the charts for Weeks Five to Eight to notice your usages of alcohol, nicotine and caffeine. Simply write down what you had, when, and how it made you feel. Try not to beat yourself up about it, nor to be jocular about it, try just to start to notice. Many offices are coffee-cultures. The only way of stopping for a break, the only way of starting a conversation, the only way of having a reason to move around, is to make tea or coffee. If this is so for you, simply become aware of it.

If you work in medicine or education, or you operate

machinery, or work in a laboratory, or drive a great deal at work, lunchtime drinking is probably taboo. But in many companies there is an ambiguous attitude to alcohol. Giving one another alcoholic drinks may be the only way anyone has of being nice to one another, and commiseration about hangovers may be an important corporate bonding ritual. It is easy in this kind of situation to begin to find one's choices about drinking become blurred. Notice how drink at work works for you, and also drink away from work.

If you smoke cigarettes, you will find that the environments in which you are allowed to smoke are becoming fewer and fewer; this may lead you frantically to 'top up' with nicotine in the car, or at home, or in ante-rooms. Just notice how much you smoke, and when, and how it makes you feel.

Maybe you do not use any of these three drugs. If not, simply use this four weeks of lifestyle to think through how much exercise with a small 'e' – walking, stair-climbing, child-lifting, bike-riding and so forth – you do each day, and how it makes you feel.

For Weeks Nine to Twelve, use the Lifestyle section of the chart to take the temperature of your own self-perception every day. Every day, either:

- write down 6 adjectives which describe you today; or
- write a sentence which describes you today; or
- write yourself a 'postcard' – a message of not more than fifteen words – saying what you feel you need to do, or achieve, or think about today. At the end of the four weeks you will have a kind of running commentary of how you perceived yourself, how you felt about yourself, during the month. Look at it and see if you notice any patterns: what are the ups and downs, the ebbs and flows cross-referencing to?

When you have completed the twelve weeks of Project One, take stock and say a big 'Well done' to yourself. You will be fitter, better toned and more flexible. You will know how to use both breathing and muscular relaxation for stress management. You will be far more self-aware.

Now you are ready to move on into Project Two.

42 Fit To Work

PROJECT 1

Cardio	Flexibility	Toning	Relaxation	Comment

WEEK 1

| Walk for 10 mins 3 times ☐ ☐ ☐ | Spend 10 mins learning basic stretching, 3 times ☐ ☐ ☐ | Learn basic toning (p. 28) 3 × 10 mins ☐ ☐ ☐ | Learn and practise abdominal breathing, 3 sessions ☐ ☐ ☐ | |

WEEK 2

| Walk for 10 mins 3 times ☐ ☐ ☐ | Spend 10 mins learning basic stretching, 3 times ☐ ☐ ☐ | Do basic toning, 10 reps per exercise, 3 sessions ☐ ☐ ☐ | Learn and practise breathing, 3 sessions ☐ ☐ ☐ | |

WEEK 3

| Walk for 10 mins twice ☐ ☐ Do 5 mins other cardio work ☐ | Do basic stretches for 10 mins, 3 sessions ☐ ☐ ☐ | Do basic toning, 10 reps per exercise, 3 sessions ☐ ☐ ☐ | Learn & practise abdominal breathing, 3 sessions ☐ ☐ ☐ | |

Cardio	Flexibility	Toning	Relaxation	Comment

WEEK 4

| Walk for 10 mins twice ☐ ☐ Do 5 mins other cardio work ☐ | Do basic stretching for 10 mins, 3 times ☐ ☐ ☐ | Do basic toning, 10 reps per exercise, 3 sessions ☐ ☐ ☐ | Learn and practise savasana (p. 37), 3 sessions ☐ ☐ ☐ | |

WEEK 5

| Walk for 10 mins once ☐ Do two other 5-minute cardio sessions ☐ ☐ | Do basic stretching and learn vars. 1 & 2 (p. 23), for 3 sessions ☐ ☐ ☐ | Do basic toning, 20 reps per exercise, and further abdominals, 3 sessions ☐ ☐ ☐ | Learn and practise savasana, 3 sessions ☐ ☐ ☐ | |

WEEK 6

| Do three 5-minute cardio sessions ☐ ☐ ☐ | Do basic stretching and learn var. 3 & 4 (p. 24), for 3 sessions ☐ ☐ ☐ | Do basic toning, 20 reps per exercise, and further abdominals, 3 sessions ☐ ☐ ☐ | Learn and practise savasana, 3 sessions ☐ ☐ ☐ | |

Cardio	Flexibility	Toning	Relaxation	Comment

WEEK 7

| Do 3 7-minute cardio sessions ☐ ☐ ☐ | Spend 15 mins stretching for 3 sessions ☐ ☐ ☐ | Basic toning, 30 reps per exercise, (15/20 for further abdominals) 3 sessions ☐ ☐ ☐ | 3 10-minute stress management sessions (p. 35) ☐ ☐ ☐ | |

WEEK 8

| Do 3 7-minute cardio sessions ☐ ☐ ☐ | Spend 15 mins stretching for 3 sessions ☐ ☐ ☐ | Basic toning 30 reps per exercise (15/20 for abs) 3 sessions ☐ ☐ ☐ | 3 10-minute stress management sessions ☐ ☐ ☐ | |

WEEK 9

| Do 3 7-minute cardio sessions ☐ ☐ ☐ | Spend 15 mins stretching for 3 sessions ☐ ☐ ☐ | Basic toning 30 reps per exercise, (15/20 for abs) 3 sessions ☐ ☐ ☐ | 3 10-minute stress management sessions ☐ ☐ ☐ | |

Cardio	Flexibility	Toning	Relaxation	Comment

WEEK 10

| Do 3 10-minute cardio sessions ☐ ☐ ☐ | Spend 15 mins stretching for 3 sessions ☐ ☐ ☐ | Basic toning 30 reps per exercise, (15/20 abs) 3 sessions ☐ ☐ ☐ | 3 10-minute stress management sessions ☐ ☐ ☐ | |

WEEK 11

| Do 3 10-minute cardio sessions ☐ ☐ ☐ | Spend 15 mins stretching and learn var. 5 (p. 26) 3 sessions ☐ ☐ ☐ | Basic toning 30 reps per exercise (15/20 abs) 3 sessions ☐ ☐ ☐ | 3 10-minute stress management sessions ☐ ☐ ☐ | |

WEEK 12

| Do 3 10-minute cardio sessions ☐ ☐ ☐ | Do all your stretches in 3 15-minute sessions ☐ ☐ ☐ | Basic toning 30 reps per exercise (15/20 abs) 3 sessions ☐ ☐ ☐ | 3 10-minute stress management sessions ☐ ☐ ☐ | |

PROJECT 1: LIFESTYLE

WEEKS 1–4: *Think about and notice what and how you eat*
Notes:

WEEKS 5–8: *Notice how and when you use alcohol, nicotine, and caffeine*
Notes:

WEEKS 9–12: *Six adjectives which describe you, or*
a sentence which describes you, or
a postcard-message you need to hear today
(log these in as often as you can):

Project Two

Welcome to Project Two! You have established a base of fitness, body awareness, and a growing general awareness about what is going on in your life affecting your health, fitness and overall well-being.

Now we are ready to push those boundaries out a bit further, look for a higher level of fitness, a deeper ability to relax, and more insights into lifestyle.

Read the sections and the new exercises, then work through the twelve weekly charts. Instructions for exercises and activities are cross-referenced on the charts in case you need to look up how to do them.

Cardiovascular session

Now that we have established an ability to work in the training zone, and got rid of many of our fears and inhibitions about doing so, we can look at some new challenges. We are still going to aim for 3 cardiovascular sessions a week, but we are going to push it up to 20 minutes per session. To start with we will break it down into 2 chunks of 10 minutes each, but by the end of Project Two the aim is to be able to sustain 20 minutes of cardiovascular exercise which takes your pulse up into your training zone, 3 times a week.

Let us start, then, by looking at the charts and choosing cardiovascular training activities. Remember that this work is for *you*; it is not to pass an invisible exam (those of us who reached our professional qualifications by jumping through hoops tend, in a manner after Pavlov's dogs, to go on jumping through imaginary hoops long after the real hoops stop, and furthermore to imagine that *every* activity in our lives involves jumping through hoops even when it clearly does not). It is not to meet a set of external standards either. It is genuinely to evolve your own internal standards and to try to meet them. This is the real core lesson of fitness, health and well-being. When you stop doing things with your body in order to get another certificate, or please the ghost of a parent or games teacher, or get a bit of praise from a current instructor, or a bit of admiration from partners and friends, then you really *are* on the way to fitness and health. All those things are fun, or pleasant, or rewarding, but they are not really the central reason for exploring your capacity for being strong and well. With that in mind, what type of cardiovascular activities are you going to choose? You could walk, jog, cycle, skip or dance aerobically. What suits you? If brisk walking is what suits you best, it is fine to do that for the whole of your cardiovascular section. With your shoulders relaxed and your back long, be aware of originating the step in your hip, not your knee. Let your arms swing naturally. This will give you the maximum benefit from walking.

Jogging and aerobic dancing must be done in properly designed and well-fitting training shoes, otherwise you risk injuries in your feet, knees, hips, or back. Although trainers are expensive, they are a good investment and will last several months if you look after them.

With cycling and skipping, to get the best benefits, remember your posture, and keep your spine and abdomen lifting and your shoulders relaxed throughout your session.

In all cardiovascular training, avoid getting into a situation where you are gasping for breath. You should be able to talk or sing without tension while you are exercising.

In Weeks One and Two, do 10 minutes of your chosen activity with your pulse in the training zone, then have a two or three minute rest during which you keep moving gently and slowly. Now do another 10 minutes in your training zone, either in the same activity, or another of the cardiovascular ones. Fit in three sessions during the week, tick them on the chart, and then record your comments: anything at all about how you feel it is going.

During Weeks Three and Four, sustain the first burst of cardiovascular training for 15 minutes. Following this, have 2 or 3 minutes' rest during which you keep moving slowly and gently. Then do 5 more minutes of either the same or an alternative cardiovascular activity. Follow this pattern for 3 sessions per week. Tick the sessions off on the charts and record your comments too.

On Week Five, keep your brisk walk, or your jogging, dancing, cycling, or skipping, going for a continuous 20 minutes. Do not get out of breath; adjust your pace to stay within the training zone.

When you stop, think back to the early weeks of Project One and your first painful efforts at cardiovascular development. Take time to feel really pleased at how far you have come!

Do three 20-minute bursts of cardiovascular training per week for Weeks Five, Six and Seven. Vary the activities as much as you like, or do the same one each time – whatever feels right for you. Enjoy your endurance and your ability to work up a good sweat with control, without getting into a panic. Record your sessions and comments on the charts.

Week Eight is a watershed week in all five of our disciplines in Project Two. It is a time to have a think about where you might want to take that particular discipline away from the framework of the Projects. What you will probably find is that some of the disciplines are a bit of a chore, but one or two really catch your imagination and you start feeling that you would like to take them further. The Projects are deliberately designed so that you do not need any special equipment and you could do it all at home (or from your home, in the case of jogging round the park for example). Now you might in some cases think about activities which do need equipment or membership of a class or club. Look on Week Eight as the moment on the motorway when the countdown flashes appear for a turn-off. Maybe you want to take one of those roads.

What roads might a growing enthusiasm for cardiovascular training make you want to take? You might have an increasing affection for running and want to join a harriers' club and train in company for sprints, longer runs, cross-countries, and even marathons. Once you can jog regularly and comfortably for 20 minutes at a time, you can go and join such a club with enough baseline fitness to get started without embarrassment.

You might enjoy the experience of working up a good sweat

and join a health club where there are a range of different facilities for doing so, such as exercise bikes and running machines, step exercises, versa climbers, and rowing machines. These types of machines improve in design and complexity all the time, and can provide you with hill programmes, interval training, and all kinds of variations to challenge you further.

Now that you know you can get through 20 minutes in the training zone without any tension, you can confidently join an aerobic, jazz dance, or any other fast-pace dance class, knowing that even if you do have to stop for rests from time to time at first, you basically have the fitness level there to get you through such a class without panicking.

Finally, there might be a team sport, a racquet sport or an activity such as climbing, rambling or hiking, which you used to enjoy years ago, but have felt too unfit to take part in for some time. Obviously there is still a step to make to get yourself from, say, an ability to do 20 minutes' cardiovascular training to an ability to play a hard team sport for 40 minutes each way, but, again, you have broken the back of getting the fitness level back again.

Think about it. Do you want to go along one of those roads? If so, begin to make enquiries about how to do so. Keep your 20 minutes, 3 times a week, going while you do. Check them off in the boxes, and record your intentions and progress in the comments section as you go along. If you join a club, class, or team, and train or play vigorously with them, begin to record those as cardiovascular sessions. If there are less than three a week, top up with plain at-home cardiovascular work as before. Take pleasure in your widening horizons!

If cardiovascular work does not particularly turn you on or point you in any obvious further directions, just continue maintaining 20 minutes training, 3 times a week, checking it off in the boxes, and noting down any comments. If you want to, you can push this a bit further when you come to Project Three; if you do not want to, keeping up this level of activity will keep you cardiovascularly fit and well.

Flexibility

One of the joys of starting a flexibility programme when you are relatively stiff is that you make progress in leaps and bounds. If you have done your stretch sessions 3 times a week for 12 weeks, you have probably opened up doors in your body that you had thought were jammed shut forever. Now let us take it further.

In this Project you are going to spend 20 minutes, 3 times a week stretching. Keep these as separate sessions if you like, or add them together with cardiovascular, or toning, or stress management/relaxation training if you like. If you stack them all together you will have 3 substantial one-and-a-half-hour workouts per week. You may prefer to have six lots of 40 minutes, or 12 lots of 20 minutes. Do not be worried about how to fit it all in. You can find 20- or 40-minute spots in the lunch hour, or in the after-work slot, or, if you are a person who wakes up feeling terrific, in the early morning. You already know you are reaping the benefits of growing fitness and wellness, so will not be defeated by a point of planning, far more quickly solved than most of the logistical problems you deal with every day at work.

Keep the structure of your stretching session as before – always include at least one forward bend, a side bend, a back bend, a leg stretching exercise and a twist. There are 8 new stretches to learn in this Project. Learn them, one a week as shown on the charts. Incorporate them as you go along, in combinations which please you, into your basic programme.

Remember how important it is to move into the stretches smoothly and slowly and out of the stretches smoothly and slowly. Breathe steadily in the stretches and hold them for 20 to 30 seconds. Never bounce in a stretch, and never let your ego or anything else induce you to stretch beyond your own personal maximum from stretch into strain. The only injuries I have ever had while stretching have been either when I went too far to impress somebody watching, or went too far simply because I believed I *ought* to be able to get a bit further. Listen to your body all the time, and nothing else, and you will never hurt yourself.

Here are the new stretches.

1 'Dog pose' (*adho mukha svanasana*) is a lovely stretch from

yoga. Both upper and lower body benefit, but build it into your programme as a leg-stretching exercise.

Kneel on the floor, toes tucked under, knees and feet hip-distance apart. Sit back onto your heels and stretch your hands and arms straight ahead in front of you along the floor. Inch your finger tips along the floor as far as they will go. Flatten and broaden your back. Exhaling, go onto all fours, taking most of your weight into your hands, then swing your hips up into the air and swing your weight back to the centre. You are in an inverted V position – heels stretching down towards the floor. Lift your abdomen, drop your head between your forearms, and broaden and flatten your back. Keep your soles and your palms strong and your weight lifting up into the hips.

Keep your face and throat soft, and breathe steadily. When you are ready to come down, on an exhalation gently lower your knees to the floor, tuck your feet under and sit back onto your heels, stretch forwards and stretch your hands and arms along the floor.

2 This is another leg and hip stretch. It helps you to increase the range of movement in your hip joints. Kneel up with your knees together and your feet apart. Gently sit down between your feet. Lace your fingers together and push your palms up towards the ceiling. Relax your shoulders and smooth your face. Lift your abdomen and open your chest. Breathe steadily.

If it is difficult to lower your hips to the floor, place one or more cushions between your feet making a high enough lift until you can sit down without strain. If necessary, straighten one leg in front, and only have one tucked behind. As your joints become more flexible you can remove the cushions one at a time, until you finally reach the floor.

When you are ready to finish, slowly and smoothly lower your arms, and gently straighten out your legs. If you did the stretch with one leg tucked behind and one leg straight, do it again the other way round.

3 This third new stretch counts as a forward bend in terms of

your planning, although, as you will feel, it is working legs and hips as well.

Sitting down, stretch your left leg out in front and point your left toes up to the ceiling, bend your right knee out to the side and tuck your right heel into your perineum. Sit tall, lifting your abdomen and relaxing your shoulders. On an exhalation stretch forwards towards your left foot. Either loop a belt or scarf round your left foot to help you move yourself forwards, or, if you can, hold on around your ankle or heel. Keep the front of your body long as well as keeping your back long. It is better to stretch 2 inches forwards in the correct form than to go 2 feet forwards with a hunched back and a crumpled abdomen. Breathe steadily in the stretch.

When you are ready, inhale and come up, and, exhaling, gently straighten out your legs.

Do the stretch to the other side, just as carefully and correctly, for the same length of time.

4   The fourth stretch is a forward bend too. Sit tall, stretch your left leg out in front of you, point your left toes to the ceiling. Keeping your knees together, tuck your right foot around behind you, so that it is close to your bottom. If you need cushions under your hips to make this possible for you, use them.

Sitting tall, breathe in and, exhaling, stretch forwards along the straight leg. Hook a belt or scarf around the left foot if you need it. If not, hold onto the ankle or heel. Observe all the same form about keeping your back flat and your abdomen long; do not be tempted to hunch your back to bring your nose to your knee. Visualize instead taking the top of your head towards the top of your left foot. Try to keep equal weight in each hip. If you are rolling to the right, use your elbows on the floor to even up. Breathe steadily in the stretch.

When you are ready, breathe in and come up; exhaling, gently unbend your legs. Now do the stretch to the other side, paying just as much attention to correct form, and taking the same amount of time.

5   Here is an additional twisting stretch to put into your 'vocabulary' of stretches.

Sit tall, abdomen lifting and shoulders relaxed. Straighten your left leg in front and bend your right knee, putting your right foot flat on the floor next to your left thigh.

Turning to your right, bring your left armpit to the right of your right knee. Open the palm of your left hand, facing outwards. Exhaling, stretch your right arm in an arc round behind you, bringing it to rest a foot behind you, level with your spine. Look over your right shoulder, sit tall, keep your weight in your hips (do not drop it all through the back hand). Get your open chest round as far to the right as you can. Hold the twists, breathing steadily, with your face soft and relaxed. When you are ready, inhaling, gently untangle yourself, then twist, equally carefully, the other way.

6   Here is a strong standing stretch. For the purposes of programming, count it as a side stretch.

Do this stretch for an equal length of time on both sides.

7   Count this as a side stretch too – it is a strong stretch which activates and mobilizes the whole body.

Do it to both sides. If you are pregnant, or have raised blood pressure, have your hands palm to palm in front of your heart, rather than overhead.

8 The next extra stretch is *shoulderstand*. As a child, you probably spent time quite happily upside-down. You probably spent the final weeks before your birth topsy-turvy and head-down rather than head-up. As an adult, unless you are a gymnast, a tumbler or a high-diving person, you probably do not have a lot of time upside-down. It is greatly liberating to rediscover upside-down experiences, but if you have any misgivings about doing so on your own, listen to your instincts and give it a miss for now. If you *would* like to do so, get yourself up in easy stages like this.
When you get up, lift and lighten your abdomen, and relax your jaw.

When you are confident and relaxed, try smoothly lowering your feet down behind your head – this gives a wonderful stretch to back, hips, and legs. If that gets easy, bend your legs and bring your knees into your ears. Suddenly you are close to parts of yourself you never expected to confront quite like this!

Now you have eight additional stretches to mix into your stretching sessions whenever you want them.

Look at Week Eight – the watershed week. Maybe stretching is just a piece of body maintenance for you, nothing more. If so, continuing to do 20 minutes 3 times a week will perform that function well. You can find more variety in Project Three if you want it. Keeping up this standard of flexibility will both improve your technique and help to safeguard you against injury in any physical activity you undertake.

What if you are finding stretching interesting, though, and want to pursue it further for its own sake? Many dance centres/

health clubs have a 'stretch and tone' type of class which provides an opportunity to develop your flexibility further.

You might feel drawn to yoga, an ancient and multi-faceted Eastern discipline. Most study of yoga done in the West begins in a class which consists mainly of stretching exercises (*asanas*) and breathing exercises (*pranayamas*). The discipline extends to many other aspects eventually, including philosophy, codes of conduct, dietary guidelines, and meditation techniques. For a Western person it is very useful that you can enter yoga through *asana* and *pranayama* and spread into other areas if and when you are ready. You will certainly improve your flexibility manyfold, and learn many valuable relaxation techniques if you attend a yoga class.

Choose a class with a calm non-competitive atmosphere, where the teacher walks around adjusting and encouraging the students rather than simply 'performing' at the front all the time. Yoga classes vary enormously in style and atmosphere (there are at least five major different styles of yoga being taught currently in the UK). If the first one you visit does not have the 'feel' you want, have the courage of your convictions and try others until you find the one in which you feel at home.

If you do go to a yoga or a stretch class, count it as one of your 'stretch' sessions each week. Try to do 2 other lots of 20 minutes' stretching on your own too. Remember to fill in the comments boxes with news about your progress or notes about the classes you are taking.

Toning

Your muscles will now be a little stronger, and a little more clearly defined than they were three months ago. You will probably feel better co-ordinated because your body is working more coherently as a single mechanism, and you may find your clothes are a little looser if your abdomen, hips, arms or legs were inclined to be soft and flabby before but have since firmed up.

Now let us take this a stage further with more challenging and additional toning exercises. Take the time frame up to 3 lots of 20 minutes a week, take the reps up to 24 on the exercises you already know. With the new ones, start with 10 (or your own maximum if that is less than 10), and work your way up to 20 by Week Eight if you can. Do not force or strain, but when you get to a point where you would like to stop with an exercise, try out doing 2 more reps. The self-disciplines required are interesting and paradoxical: it takes self-control not to push yourself to the point of injury, but it takes self-control to work up to your maximum potential too. The point of balance in between is a point of self-knowledge about both your body and your temperament.

Arms and upper body

Add these to your current framework of toning exercises.

1 ARM CIRCLES

   Stand with your feet hip distance apart, knees relaxed. Tuck your tailbone under, lift your abdomen, lift the crown of your head and relax your shoulders.
   Stretch your arms straight out to the sides at shoulder level. Turn your palms up towards the ceiling. Now make rapid circles with the whole of both straight arms – 10 forwards, 10 backwards. Your arms will tend to float forwards: keep them straight out to the sides.
   Move straight on: bend your wrists so that your finger tips point to the floor; arms are still straight out to the side. Curve the fingers into a loose fist. Do 10 arm circles forwards, and 10 back.
   Finally, arms still extended to the sides, grasp an imaginary door knob in each hand, and turn it one way and then the other 10 times.

2 TRICEPS EXERCISE

   The triceps muscle runs along the back of your upper arm. This exercise particularly helps to tone it.

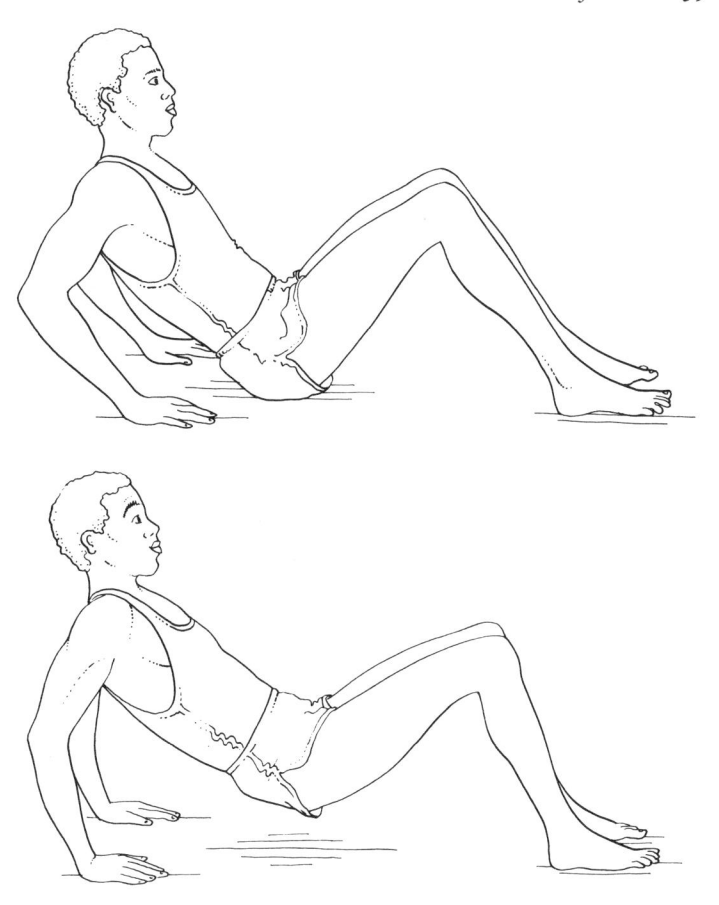

Sit on the floor, legs out in front of you and bent at the knee, feet flat on the floor. Lean back a little (keep your abdomen lifting) and place your hands on the floor 30/40 cm behind your hips, fingers pointing to your heels.

On an exhalation, slowly straighten your arms as far as you can, and lift your hips off the floor. On the inhalation, slowly and with control, lower your hips to the floor again. Do this 10 times.

3 PRESS-UP WALK

Get into the 'up' press-up position, feet 2 feet apart, hands more than shoulder-distance apart. Lift the abdomen and keep the body straight. Pivoting on your toes, walk your hands 2 steps to the left, then come back to the centre, then 2 to the right, then back to the centre. Do only 5 reps of this sequence, fewer if necessary, to start with. You will feel it working your arms and chest.

Finish by dropping to all fours, then sitting back on your hands and stretching your arms straight along the floor in front of you.

Abdominals

1 BICYCLES

Lie on the floor on your back. Press your abdomen back towards your spine and curl your pubic bone up. Bend your left knee up onto your chest, extend your right leg away, toes pointed, a couple of inches off the floor. Lace your fingers behind your head, and, exhaling, flex your abdomen back and lift your right elbow up towards your left knee.

Change: right knee bent on chest, left leg out straight, left elbow to right knee. Your head stays up, your abdomen stays flexed, throughout.

Do 10 repetitions alternating right and left sides. Exhale on the changes.

When you finish, hug your knees to your chest to release your lower back.

2 LOWER ABDOMINAL EXERCISE

Sit on the floor, legs straight out in front of you. Lean back and place your hands more than shoulder-distance apart, behind your hips, fingers pointing to your heels.

Draw your knees into your chest, feet off the floor, balancing on your hips and hands. Exhaling, stretch your legs straight ahead, 18 inches or so off the floor. Draw your knees in, then stretch your legs out 10 times altogether, fewer at first if necessary.

When you finish, lie on your back and hug your knees onto your chest.

Legs and hips

1 LEG RAISE VARIATION

Lie on your left side, support yourself on your left elbow and forearm out to the left, and your right hand on the floor in front of you.

Bend both knees to a 90 degree angle and move them forwards so your balance is still stable. Keeping your feet together, slowly lift the right knee up as far as you can, then, with control, lower it to just above the left knee again. Do 5 reps, then bring the right knee towards the chest, then return it to the start position. Do 5 of these, before turning onto your right side and doing 5 up, 5 across with the left leg. This exercise tones both your thighs and your hips.

2 LEG SWING

Start on all fours, hands shoulder-distance apart, knees hip-distance apart. Lift your abdomen. Stretch your right leg straight out to the side at right angles to your body. Raise it slowly to hip height, then slowly lower the toe almost to the floor. Do 10 on the right side, then change and do 10 on the left. Finish by going back onto all fours, sitting back on your heels, then stretching your arms and hands out in front of you along the floor.

You will feel that this exercise also works both thighs and hips.

3 BOTTOM SQUEEZING

This works hips and thighs too, but in this case the emphasis is very much on the bottom.

Lie on your back on the floor with your knees bent and feet a little more than hip-distance apart. Press the back of your waist into the floor and curl your pubic bone up towards your navel. Exhaling, continue that movement so that your hips lift up into the air. Inhale, lower your hips almost to the floor but not quite; exhaling, lift your hips up and at the same time press your knees together. Inhale, lower your hips and part your knees. Exhale, raise your hips and close your knees. Do 10 of these squeezes, or, if you need to, fewer to start off with. Do not despair – the things that seemed impossible 12 weeks ago seem easy now, and the same will happen with this in time.

Incorporate these extra exercises into your toning programme, and, adding a couple of reps as and when you can, see if you can get yourself up to 24 reps for everything except the Press-Up Walk by Week Eight.

Week Eight is thinking-about-development time, and if toning particularly appeals to you in itself, you might very well want to think about starting to do some resistance training with weights. We are doing toning work in these projects by asking our muscles to move part of our own body-weight around, because we specifically want to create a fitness system which requires no equipment and can be done anywhere. If you find toning work interesting and exhilarating and you want to take it further, you can make your body work even harder by using weights which increase the work your muscles do even more. Muscles grow in response to demand. Give them more to do, in a structured and organized way, and they will grow larger and stronger in order to be able to do it. Join in a gymnasium or health club with clean, well-maintained weight machines and a selection of free weights. Make sure that they will do a careful assessment of your present fitness level and that they will design a personal programme for you. Furthermore make sure that a qualified instructor will induct you thoroughly on how to use all the equipment, and that somebody qualified is in attendance at all times so that you can ask questions while you are working out.

If the first gym you look at falls down on any one of those criteria, look around for somewhere else. Think about the atmosphere as well: is it a place where you will enjoy spending time?

Well-programmed, well-carried out weight training programmes can literally re-sculpt your body, which can be extremely exciting.

Alternatively, you might enjoy the 'stretch and tone' or 'body-sculpting' type of studio class, where exercises using your own body weight, plus ankle and wrist weights, small hand-weights, 'dyna-bands', and so on, are used to create pleasantly defined contours in the body.

If you attend class, or work-out with weights at the gym, count those as the appropriate number of toning sessions on the charts. If for some reason you have to miss class or the gym, do the Project Two toning exercises at home instead. Remember to fill in your comments too.

If toning exercises do not particularly appeal to you, simply continue with your three 20 minute sessions per week to keep yourself feeling lighter and tighter in a pleasant way.

Stress management and relaxation

In Weeks One and Two of Project Two we will learn and practise another very useful form of breathing discipline: alternate nostril breathing. We will spend a little time on that and a little time in *savasana*, so that in fact you will only need 10 minutes on this section 3 times a week. Add it on to the end of one of the other sessions if you like, or do it in bed before you go to sleep. Do remember to have enough warm layers on so that you will not feel chilled in *savasana*.

Alternate nostril breathing

- Sit cross-legged on the floor. If you are tired support your back against the wall or some other stable support. Lift your abdomen and relax your shoulders.

- Place your left hand on your left knee. Place the middle finger of your right hand on the 'third eye' position, between your eyebrows and up a little, and check that you can close your right nostril with your thumb and your left nostril with your fourth finger. When you do this breathing, use the minimum pressure possible to close each nostril.

1. Inhale.* Close your right nostril with your thumb, exhale through the left.
2. Inhale through the left.
3. Close the left nostril with your fourth finger and take your thumb away from the right.
4. Exhale through the right.
5. Inhale through the right.*

- Repeat the cycle from * to * several times. From time to time, check your posture, ensuring that your spine and abdomen are lifting, that the back of your neck is long, that your shoulders are relaxed. Let your eyes close.

- Let the breath become slow and deep. Do not rush.

- When you are ready to stop, float your right hand away from your face down onto your knee. Blink your eyes open gently to let in the light.

- Without disturbing yourself too much, lie down for 5 minutes of *savasana*.

You can use alternate nostril breathing as a way of controlling panic and anxiety and it is a very great help if you have restless insomnia. (You do not have to sit up; do it lying down in bed.) Steadying the breath steadies the spirit too. It can be done unobtrusively at an office desk, or in a few minutes locked in the loo if you need to collect yourself away from your colleagues!

In Weeks Three and Four we will learn and practise another discipline which is very helpful in managing stress. It is the preliminary stage in meditation: simply, clearing the mind. Do not at this stage set yourself a target amount of time to spend on this or you will get all knotted up about whether you can do it for long enough. In fact it will be 10 minutes *maximum* at first, so that is the period of time you need to set aside.

Clearing the mind

Read this through and assimilate this, then try it out.

- Find a comfortable sitting position, and as always check that you have equal weight in each hip, spine and abdomen lifting, back of the neck long, and shoulders relaxed. Be still. Breathe a little more deeply and a little more slowly than usual. Hear the breath coming and going.

- Now, as though you were tuning into a radio station, tune into what is going on in your own mind. Simply observe it. The chances are that it is pretty hectic in there. Clear thoughts, diffuse thoughts, anxieties, things to remember, new ideas, opinions, and so forth are jostling around and ricocheting off each other. Just observe.

- Now begin to think about letting those thoughts, ideas, opinions, and anxieties go. Do not force, do not strain, just let them drain away. Imagine them flowing away from you, till your mind is clear and empty. Let it all go.

- More thoughts will arise. They will float up, like bubbles in a drink. It does not matter. Simply observe each thought, and let it go. Do not tense up. It is not a competition or a race, it is just a thing you are learning. Let each thought go.

- There will be a natural length of time for you to spend on this. Just spend that amount of time. At first it will be a small number of minutes: this is fine. When you have had enough, gently stop. Let your mind return to its everyday state (though it will, inevitably, be quieter than before). Blink your eyes open slowly to let in the light. Do not rush. Move slowly back into the activities of the day.

Practise this technique 3 times in Week Three and 3 times in Week Four. Tick the boxes and note down in the comment boxes how you are getting on.

In Weeks Five and Six take on board yet another way of working through stress and getting in touch with inner resources of calm: this time it is guided fantasy.

Guided fantasy

There is no 'correct' way to respond to a guided fantasy. It is just a way of freeing up the valuable and creative resources of your intuitive and subconscious self. At work we train ourselves so hard to be objective, rigorous and empirically responsive, that our intuitive side can atrophy. The ability to flow well between the objective and the rational is a great asset. Follow this fantasy in your mind's eye and see what comes up for you.

Either tape the fantasy below, or read it through and become familiar with it, then lay yourself down in *savasana* and let it go through your mind, as slowly as you like.

It is a warm sunny day and you are walking to the woods. Feel the sun on your face and body as you walk. Notice the things you see, and the things you smell. What can you hear? What is the path like? . . .

Now you have entered the cool of the woods. What is the ground like underfoot? Be aware of the smells, the sights and the sounds as you travel through the wood. . . .

After walking a while you come upon a clearing. The sun is shining in the clearing and there is a comfortable place for you to lie down and rest. Lie down there and relax. Feel the warm sun soaking into your body, your muscles releasing and your joints softening. Be aware of what you can see and hear. What textures and what smells are there? Just be there, just rest. . . .

Now it is time to return to here and now. Float yourself in your mind's eye from the sunny clearing to the room you are in, as though on a magic carpet. Become aware of where you are, of who you are. Yawn and stretch to awaken your body, and blink your eyes open to let in the light. Let any sense of peace you found stay with you for the rest of the day. Let anything that stays in your mind from your fantasy (a particular visual image, a particular sound, whatever) stay in your mind too. It has a message for you.

Here is a different one in case you want a change.

Lie down comfortably in savasana. *Now take yourself in your mind's eye to a rocky escarpment with short, grassy turf between brown boulders, and look out over a vast plain. Be aware of what you hear, what you smell, the textures of the ground under your feet, the vast plain, and the vast sky. Storm clouds gather and there is a sudden, violent shower of rain. . . .*

When the storm is over, the warm sun warms you through. Gleams of water glitter here and there, and to the right a brilliant rainbow develops. . . .

Move towards the rainbow, and catching the ends of it, pull them together to make a giant rainbow-coloured balloon, underneath it a basket into which you can climb. . . .

Climb into the basket, making yourself lighter by throwing away anything that is weighing you down. Now you are free to float anywhere you want to in the huge landscape. . . .

Notice what you see, what you smell, what you hear. Notice what you feel. . . .

Now it is time to come back to the here and now. See your rainbow balloon float gently to the ground. Step out of it and transport yourself, as though on an invisible magic carpet, back to the floor where you are lying, the room you are in. Yawn and stretch to awaken your body, and blink your eyes open to let in the light. Let any sense of peace you found remain with you for the rest of the day. Let any vivid images or impressions from the fantasy stay with you too. They have a message for you.

Make time for a guided fantasy for 3 sessions in Week Five and 3 sessions in Week Six. Check them off on the charts and make any comments in the box.

In Week Seven, do one session of Alternate Nostril Breathing, one of Clearing the Mind, and one of Guided Fantasy.

Spend some time in Week Eight thinking about whether you want to take any of this any further, in a specializing sense.

You might feel that *savasana* is working well for you, but that residual tension in your back, neck and shoulders sometimes makes it difficult. If that is so, you might consider having a massage done by a qualified massage person at a health centre or similar. You might also consider this if you are working very

68 Fit To Work

hard physically. In a part of my life when I was teaching 5 or 6 yoga classes a week, and training several times a week in Tae Kwon Do, I made sure I had a massage once a month and felt sure that it prevented stress from accumulating in my body and injuries from occurring. If your work is hard physically or you have a full sporting schedule you may well find the same.

If you are enjoying the guided fantasy element of stress management, you could buy a couple of relaxation tapes (advertised in yoga magazines, sold in 'radical' bookshops etc.). These literally do vary from the sublime to the ridiculous, and it is a bit hit and miss selecting them: personal recommendation from a friend is probably the surest way to find one you do like. Alternatively, you could make your own, with words you evolve for yourself and music you choose.

You may be becoming interested in the breathing techniques we have been learning, and if so you may like to read more about them. Several fascinating books about breathing are listed in the Further Reading section. It is a whole world, and, as we have said before, many people devote whole lifetimes to its study. You can certainly have an enjoyable time investigating it further, and if you are fortunate you might be able to combine an interest in breathing and stretching in a yoga class which does *pranayama* (breathing exercises) as well as *asana* (postures).

Reading about stress management itself can be useful too. However, my sense is that modern and elaborate stress management techniques are struggling towards the essential skill of *detachment*. That is the key concept in Buddhism, so that, however esoteric and irrelevant it might seem at first for a modern executive to do so, you may as well go straight to the source of the idea and read some Buddhist or Zen Buddhist texts. Several are listed in Further Reading.

Detachment seems strange to us in the West, since we are so committed to engagement, involvement, taking initiatives, creating our own destiny. However, detachment is not the same as passivity. Detachment is the ability to stand back and say, 'Things are going well, and I remain calm inside', 'Things are going badly and I remain calm inside'; it is to find the paradoxical point of balance where on the one hand everything matters desperately and we must do what we can for a good outcome at all times, and on the other hand nothing matters at all. If this catches your imagination, start to read about it. If not, simply leave it.

Lastly, you may have enjoyed the 'Clearing your Mind' exercise. To take this further, we will move into meditation itself on Project Three. You might be able to find a meditation group which you could attend: either run by a yoga teacher, or if you are near a martial arts *dojo* they may have *zazen* meditation times. As with all groups and classes, follow your own instinct about whether the instruction is sound (as well, of course, as checking the credentials of the instructor) and whether the atmosphere feels right for you. Once you become familiar with meditation it is a wonderful way to refresh yourself and clear the trash out of your mind and heart, and it can be done anywhere.

Maybe you do not want to take any stress management things further at all. That is fine. Just do the 3 spots per week, and your stress levels will stabilize and then come down anyway.

Lifestyle

In Weeks One and Two of Project Two your lifestyle task is to develop yet another area of awareness, this time to do with moods. Use 10 minutes, 3 times a week, to write a short mood-diary for the preceding days. Get a sense of when the ups and downs happen, what tends to trigger them, and how you felt. This is an awareness exercise, not a judging exercise. The point is to look at how extensive or otherwise the fluctuations are, and what the significant affecting factors are.

In the last session on Week Two, look back through your notes, and see if you can make for yourself 2 or 3 action points. Action points, to be any use to anyone, have to be specific and they have to be achievable. If a particular person, or a particular item of work (phone calls with difficult clients, etc.) regularly makes you panic, plan to intercept your panic with an exhalation and a calming message to yourself next time. If you always get depressed at lunch time because you feel bored and lonely, so you go to the pub with the others, drink too much, and have a rotten afternoon, aim for at least one lunch hour next week where you do something specific and positive for yourself: go for a swim, read a good book, take a walk in the park. If certain people or certain activities always cheer you up and leave you on a high, think of a specific and achievable way you could have a little more of them next week.

In Weeks Three and Four take 3 lots of 10 minutes to think about how you are using your time. Work out the following things:

- How many hours a week do you spend doing paid work?
- How many hours a week do you spend doing unpaid work? (This includes housework, childcare, shopping, unpaid overtime.)
- How many hours a week do you spend having fun?

Look carefully at these numbers and ask yourself whether they reflect the kind of balance you want in your life. If they do, fine. If not, begin to consider what you want to do about it. These are 'seeing the wood for the trees' questions. We may get into single-minded pursuit of money and success, and then suddenly notice with alarm that we barely see our children and that when we do, we are so tired that we cannot play with them or chat with them. We may spend many, many hours a week doing unpaid work without even noticing it, then wonder why we feel so drained. It may be important to look at streamlining all unpaid work to a minimum, and delegating as much of it as we can.

Many, many adults have almost no fun! This is one of the horrible consequences of managing multiple commitments while going through a multiple recession. Do consider, too, whether 'fun' for you is always represented by getting smashed on one or other of society's acceptable drugs. Although the occasional Dionysiac binge is arguably all right, things really are not in good balance when that is our only way of enjoying ourselves. We also need to be able to laugh and frolic in other ways.

Think through your data and see if you can come up with two or three action points regarding the balance of the way you use your time. Make them specific and achievable. Give yourself a realistic target time on them too, so that you commit yourself to *when* you will have made some changes.

In Weeks Five and Six we are going to do an exercise called 'Contact your Strength'. You have six 10-minute spots to spend on this over the 2 Weeks. Plan when to have them, check them off on the charts, and note down your comments.

Contact your strength

Growing up in this culture, on the whole we expect to get our validations from other people. We look to parents, teachers and bosses for affirmations of our worth, and for exam results, promotions and the admiration of our partners to feed our self-esteem.

There is an obvious logical flaw in this behaviour, which is that other people can always, for one reason or another, withdraw their validation, and there are times when the most spectacular exam results or pay rise means nothing at all in the long dark midnight of the soul!

This is where 'contacting your strength' comes in. If you can, a little bit at a time, build up a sense of appropriate and flexible self-esteem on the inside. Then, the opinion of those on the outside and its unpredictability matters less.

Begin by making a list for yourself which goes like this:

In the last year I have

learned:

survived:

helped someone else to:

made:

enjoyed:

Make this list as full as you can. You will probably be surprised at just how much you have got through in the last year.

In your next session start to make a list of your strengths, the things you are good at. Draw on the information you pulled together about your activities in the last 12 months. Include everything, however apparently trivial. It all counts, it all enriches you. It is all amazingly transferable too: for instance, periods of endurance in your private life provide you with a great depth of courage to exercise at work, and skills like designing a beautiful garden develop both creativity and planning ability.

In the following lifestyle time, review your list of strengths and allow yourself to feel pleased about them. There are probably one or two of which you feel really proud. Focus on those one or two and get very clearly in touch with what they are.

Those three focusing sessions take you through Week Five.

In Week Six, you do not spend set-aside time on Contact Your Strength, but you begin to put it into action. Whenever a tense or fraught situation happens, whenever you feel undermined, or threatened, or challenged, exhale and tune into the area of strength you have chosen of which you feel particularly proud. *Then* make your response. The first few times you do this it will feel odd and artificial, but it will soon feel natural. It is a simple but effective way of empowering yourself.

Continue to do this during Week Seven as well, and remember to note in the comment space any effect it is having.

During Week 8 you take the lifestyle time as a period of reflection on what has gone before. You have raised your level of awareness about eating and drinking, about emotional patterns, about time management, and about contacting your strength. Take time to work out whether there is any action you want to take on any of these. It might take the form of trying out a more vegetarian diet, or aiming for a number of alcohol-free days a week. It might involve undertaking some specific training (for example, many organizations make a Time Management course available to their personnel), or it could be that there is some kind of developmental group you would like to join. Now, your toes may curl up at the very thought, and certainly it would be fair to say that the 1980s spawned thousands of self-help groups for every condition and preoccupation under the sun, not all of them well run or of any positive use to their members. Nevertheless, support or development groups, be they men's groups, women's groups, menopause groups, alcoholics' support groups, co-counselling groups, therapy groups, whatever, may be of great and significant use to you at certain points in your life. If there is a particular aspect of life you want to explore, or a particular condition you want support and sharing for, track down a group that will be useful to you.

Make any action points time-targeted, allowing yourself the next four weeks, Weeks Nine, Ten, Eleven, and Twelve, to get them into place.

PROJECT 2

Cardio	Flexibility	Toning	Relaxation	Comment

WEEK 1

| 10 mins – rest – 10 mins, 3 sessions ☐ ☐ ☐ | 20 mins stretch, 3 sessions ☐ ☐ ☐

learn dog pose (p. 51) ☐ | 24 reps per exercise, 3 sessions ☐ ☐ ☐

learn new exercise 1 (p. 58) ☐ | Learn and practise alternate nostril breathing (p. 63)

☐ ☐ ☐ | |

WEEK 2

| 10 mins – rest – 10 mins, 3 sessions ☐ ☐ ☐ | 20 mins stretch, 3 sessions ☐ ☐ ☐

learn new stretch 2 (p. 52) ☐ | 24 reps per exercise ☐ ☐ ☐

learn new exercise 2 (p. 58) ☐ | Learn and practise alternate nostril breathing

☐ ☐ ☐ | |

WEEK 3

| 15 mins – rest – 5 mins, 3 sessions ☐ ☐ ☐ | 20 mins stretch, 3 sessions ☐ ☐ ☐

learn new stretch 3 (p. 52) ☐ | 24 reps per exercise (p.59) ☐ ☐ ☐

learn new exercise 3 (p. 59) ☐ | Clearing the mind (p. 65)

☐ ☐ ☐ | |

Cardio	Flexibility	Toning	Relaxation	Comment

WEEK 4

| 3 × 20 mins ☐ ☐ ☐ | 20 mins stretch, 3 sessions ☐ ☐ ☐ learn new stretch 4 (p. 53) ☐ | 24 reps per exercise ☐ ☐ ☐ learn new exercise 4 (p. 60) ☐ | Clearing the mind ☐ ☐ ☐ | |

WEEK 5

| 3 × 20 mins ☐ ☐ ☐ | 20 mins stretch, 3 sessions ☐ ☐ ☐ learn new stretch 5 (p. 54) ☐ | 24 reps per exercise ☐ ☐ ☐ learn new exercise 5 (p. 60) ☐ | Guided fantasy ☐ ☐ ☐ | |

WEEK 6

| 3 × 20 mins ☐ ☐ ☐ | 20 mins stretch, 3 sessions ☐ ☐ ☐ learn new stretch 6 (p. 54) ☐ | 24 reps per exercise ☐ ☐ ☐ learn new exercise 6 (p. 61) ☐ | Guided fantasy ☐ ☐ ☐ | |

Cardio	Flexibility	Toning	Relaxation	Comment

WEEK 7

| 3 × 20 mins ☐ ☐ ☐ | 20 mins stretch, 3 sessions ☐ ☐ ☐ learn new stretch 8 (p. 55) ☐ | 24 reps per exercise ☐ ☐ ☐ learn new exercise 7 (p. 61) ☐ | Alternate nostril breathing ☐ Clearing the mind ☐ Guided fantasy | |

WEEK 8

| 3 × 20 mins ☐ ☐ ☐ Join a class or club? Notes: .... | 3 × 20 mins ☐ ☐ ☐ Join a class? Notes: .... | 24 reps per exercise ☐ ☐ ☐ learn new exercise 8 (p. 61) ☐ Join a club or class? Notes: ..... | Notes: .... | |

WEEK 9

| 3 × 20 mins ☐ ☐ ☐ or attend class or club ☐ | 3 × 20 mins ☐ ☐ ☐ or attend class ☐ | 24 reps per exercise ☐ ☐ ☐ or attend class or club ☐ | Note your chosen activity: | |

Cardio	Flexibility	Toning	Relaxation	Comment

WEEK 10

| *2 × 20 mins* ☐ ☐ ☐ | *3 × 20 mins* ☐ ☐ ☐ | *24 reps per exercise* ☐ ☐ ☐ | *Note your chosen activity:* | |
| *or attend class or club* ☐ | *or attend class* ☐ | *or attend class or club* ☐ | | |

WEEK 11

| *3 × 10 mins* ☐ ☐ ☐ | *3 × 20 mins* ☐ ☐ ☐ | *24 reps per exercise* ☐ ☐ ☐ | *Note your chosen activity:* | |
| *or attend class or club* ☐ | *or attend class* ☐ | *or attend class or club* ☐ | | |

WEEK 12

| *3 × 20 mins* ☐ ☐ ☐ | *3 × 20 mins* ☐ ☐ ☐ | *24 reps per exercise* ☐ ☐ ☐ | *Note your chosen activity:* | |
| *or attend class or club* ☐ | *or attend class* ☐ | *or attend class or club* ☐ | | |

78 Fit To Work

PROJECT 2: LIFESTYLE

WEEKS 1 & 2: *Brief mood diary.*

WEEKS 3 & 4:
Hours per week paid work:

Hours per week unpaid work:

Hours per week fun:

WEEKS 5, 6 & 7: *See p. 71 'Contact Your Strength'.*
WEEK 8: *Review: see p. 72.*
weeks 9–12: *Planning: see p. 73.*

Project Three

Now it is time to start on Project Three. If you started at the beginning of the book, six months have passed by now. If you began at Project Two, you are twelve weeks along. You are much better acquainted with your body, have greater confidence in your ability to develop its capacity, and have done a great deal of work on thinking creatively about your way of life in a positive and holistic manner.

Welcome to Project Three! Here we learn some interesting new exercises, and increase our fitness and awareness levels even more. Let us get straight into our new programmes.

Cardiovascular section

If you now belong to a running or cycling club, or go to a fast-pace dance or aerobic class, or play a sport which raises your pulse into the training zone for at least 30 minutes at least 3 times a week, check those off on the charts as your cardiovascular work. Do take time to be pleased that you have empowered yourself so well.

If you have preferred to do cardiovascular things on your own, here are some ways of pushing it a bit further. You are getting pretty experienced by now. Follow the charts exactly if you wish, but equally try out and do the things which particularly suit and interest you, and mix and match them into your training.

PYRAMIDS

You could incorporate pyramids into Weeks One, Two and Three of your cardiovascular training. They push you to the maximum for a short period. (You may well be training *anaerobically* for this short period, so this is not strictly speaking cardiovascular, but rather stamina training.)

Do a pyramid before your cardiovascular workout and another at the end. Start with 5 as your starting-point, but work your way up to 8 or even 10. A pyramid goes like this:

5 press-ups
followed by
5 sit-ups
followed by
5 squat-thrusts
then
4 sit-ups
followed by
4 press-ups
followed by
4 squat-thrusts

and so on down to 1. It sounds quite easy, doesn't it? You will enjoy the challenge of trying it.

FARTLEK

If you are a runner already you will know this word. If not you may think it sounds strange. However, the ear gets used to locutions once their meaning is assimilated. There is a stance in Tae Kwon Do – cat stance – which is called *boem soegi* in Korean. The pronunciation is, quite exactly, 'bum soggy'. However, you only hear it as odd once or twice. Once you know what it means and you begin to try to do it, it sounds entirely ordinary.

'Fartlek' means 'speed play', and is a type of training which consists of running at varying speeds, bursts of faster running alternating with periods of slower running to allow the body to recover. You can start to do fartlek when you know your own running ability well enough, which by now you probably do, being well past all those initial battles just to keep going for another couple of minutes, and having some idea how much running you have in your 'tank'. A useful pattern over about 2.5k would be something like:

– jog for about half a mile (to warm up)

- sprint hard for about 100m
- jog for about 150m
- sprint hard for about 100m
- jog for about 300m
- run at a medium pace for 400m
- jog for 500m
- cool down (keep walking steadily for a while).

During Weeks Four, Five and Six you might like to try out some fartlek. If you run indoors on a machine, look at some of the 'interval' and 'hill' programmes on the machine and play with these.

VARY THE TERRAIN

Varying the terrain for anyone who mainly commits themselves to running as their cardiovascular training means literally what it says.

During Weeks Seven, Eight and Nine investigate some new routes for your runs and be prepared to include some slopes, hills and even flights of steps, which will vary the pace and stamina you need.

If you run at night, wear light clothes and a luminous belt/luminous heel and elbow flashes. Be conscious of making yourself highly visible to anybody approaching you in a vehicle with lights. Women certainly, and probably men as well, need to be aware of issues of personal safety. If you run in quiet areas (even the more deserted parts of a familiar park), or are looking for new routes in unfamiliar places, sadly, you must take into account the risk of attack. Be alert, *always* listen to your intuition, and if at all possible run with a friend or a group. If you do go alone, let somebody else know where you are and when you will be back so you will be missed quickly if you do not arrive.

This is horribly restrictive and claustrophobic, but it is necessary to be realistic. If you do get attacked, fight back (see Paddy O'Brien, *Self-Defence for Everyday* (Sheldon 1992)). You are fitter now than for many months previously, and this will help you to survive.

If you are dancing, or taking part in a sport, or doing some other form of cardiovascular work, during Weeks Seven, Eight and Nine, change the terrain by, from time to time and to keep yourself fresh, doing something different. Have you thought of swimming? This could be a refreshing alternative, slotted into your day as a lunchtime or an after-work half-hour. Swimming lengths reasonably vigorously you will soon be into your training zone.

If you always go to jazz class, try belly-dancing, or some other style once in a while; if you always go to step class, try a cardio workout or aerobics from time to time.

The jet of adrenaline you get from putting yourself into an unfamiliar situation and trying something new can help you to achieve that little bit more. If you *always* do the same thing, you can become mechanical and stale. Furthermore you may, by keeping an open mind and trying something new every now and again, stumble across some type of exercise which is going to be a real and sustaining inspiration to you for years.

CIRCUIT TRAINING

Circuits certainly build both strength and stamina, and they could come in as a choice here or in the Toning Section equally well: so swap them into either as you like.

Many health clubs and gyms have a circuit class where you move rapidly around the circuit, probably varied from week to week, doing sets of sprints, press-ups, sit-ups, steps, weights, and whatever else the instructor decides to include. You have the basic fitness to do this now, and no good instructor will let you feel stupid if it is a struggle to begin with. Being with a group, having the encouragement of an instructor, and getting into a rapid rhythm, helps to spur you on into much more than you would have believed yourself capable. There are moments during any circuit class when you wonder why you have let yourself in for it, but you do feel terrific afterwards. The 'suffering together' often builds a camaraderie into the class as well.

Consider working a circuit training class into your programme during Weeks Ten, Eleven and Twelve.

Flexibility

If, by now, you attend a yoga or a stretch class, you will be discovering all sorts of extra movement in your body. Check the classes off on the charts and take time to be pleased that you are on this journey of discovery with your body.

Here are some more stretches to increase your 'vocabulary' of exercises.

SALUTES TO THE SUN AND *ASTANGA VINYASA* YOGA

A set of stretches performed in a flowing sequence can be a wonderful way of waking your flexibility up. If you are very pressed for time, do the sequence half a dozen times: it will take you five minutes and will do a great deal to promote and preserve your flexibility.

The sequence is called 'Salute to the Sun' or *Surya Namaskars* and goes like this:

Learn it slowly and carefully and perform it very accurately and with control. Alternate the foot which goes back in Step 3 each time you do the sequence. Keep the face soft, shoulders relaxed, and abdomen lifted.

Learn this sequence moving from one stretch to the other in the rhythm of your own breath. Once you are so familiar with it that you do not have to stop and think what comes next anymore, it is fun sometimes to do very briskly, and sometimes to do very slowly and thoughtfully. Learn and assimilate 'Salute to the Sun' and incorporate it into your stretch programme during Weeks One, Two and Three.

If you enjoy choreographing your stretches like this, you may particularly enjoy a branch of yoga called *Astanga Vinyasa* yoga. In this style, *all* the postures are linked together with flowing movements, forming a sequence which lasts an hour to an hour-and-a-half. The body heats up tremendously and sweats profusely. Toxins are flushed out in the sweat, and the heat allows a dramatic increase in stretchiness of muscle fibres and flexibility of joints.

MORE LEG STRETCHING

In Weeks Four, Five and Six, learn some further strong leg-stretching exercises. These exercises also do a great deal to mobilize the hip joints.

- Sit tall, on the centre of the pelvic floor, not slumped back onto your tailbone. Lift up through the spine; lift your abdomen lightly. Relax your shoulders, soften your face, and lift the crown of your head up towards the ceiling. Stretch your legs wide apart and point your toes up towards the ceiling. Take care not to fall back onto your tailbone.

- Breathing in, look over your right shoulder and slide your left hand as far as you can down your left leg. As you exhale, stretch your right arm up into the air and, exhaling, reach over the top towards your left toes. Only go as far down as you can without turning your chest towards the floor. Hold for a few seconds, breathing steadily, with your face relaxed. Breathing in come up to the centre, and, exhaling, stretch in the same way to the other side, hold the same amount of time, and, inhaling, come up to the centre. On your next exhalation, stretch forwards, walking your hands forward on the floor in front of you. Hinge at the hips and keep your back flat and your abdomen lifting, and keep the back of your neck long. It is better to go two inches forwards like this in the correct form, than to get your head onto the floor by hunching your back over and squashing your abdomen.

Incorporate this into your stretching programme during Weeks Four, Five and Six.

MORE BACK BENDS

Develop some further back bends to include in your programme. Always follow them with the forward 'praying stretch' to ease out your lower back.

- Kneel up with your knees together and your feet together. Breathing in, stretch up out of your hips. Now, emphasizing keeping your thighs vertical and a sense of your hips moving forwards, on an exhalation gently bend backwards and start to reach towards your feet. At your comfortable maximum, relax your head and neck. Hold for a few seconds, with your

86 Fit To Work

face soft, breathing steadily. When you come up, either use abdomen strength (*not* back strength) to lift yourself up centrally or if that feels risky, gently sink back onto your heels and lift your head. Relax forwards into the praying stretch.

- Try pushing up into a bridge pose: lying on your back, doubling your hands back by your shoulders and bending your knees, put your feet flat on the floor, hip-difference apart. On an exhalation, lift your hips up into the air, and if they will flow up easily, your shoulders too. Hold for a few seconds, breathing steadily, then, on an exhalation, come gently down onto the ground and hug your knees onto your chest. This is an exhilarating back bend which also gives a beautiful feeling of openness on the front surface of the body.

SPECTACULAR STRETCHES

This really is the joy of stretching! If you are getting really mobile you might like to try these (*Eka Pada Chakrasana, Kapotasana, Kurmasana*). Always move into extreme stretches like these slowly and with the outbreath. If you find yourself starting to tense up, come gently out of the attempted stretch and leave it alone for the time being. Try again in another couple of months: rushing will only lead to injury.

If you ever get stuck, relax your abdomen, steady your breathing, and work out the easy way out – there always is one. I once got stuck in *Kurmasana*, and remember thinking, absurdly, 'I shall have to phone the fire brigade'! Luckily, I remembered to let my abdomen go soft and to slow my breathing, and a few moments' reflection made it clear that all I needed to do was wriggle my feet sufficiently to ease my knees up, and then my arms would slide out from underneath them.

There is a real sense of celebration when stretching like this becomes possible. Enjoy playing with these stretches during Weeks Ten and Eleven, and if any of them are accessible to you, think back to the struggle you had in Project One Week One, and say 'Well done' to yourself!

DEEP SLOW STRETCH

In the final Week of this Project, it is useful to take yourself right back to fundamentals again. Pick half a dozen stretches from your repertoire and do them really slowly and attentively, holding them for a long time and really settling into them. This grounds or roots you back into the quality of pleasure which deep, slow stretching can give.

Toning

Weight-training people, and people attending body-sculpting class, can happily tick their sessions off on the toning charts. You are probably finding the different curves and shapes of your body very enjoyable too.

For your 'at home' sessions, you may like to add these more demanding toning exercises.

FULL PRESS-UPS

- Lie on the floor on your abdomen, feet 2 feet apart and hands 4 inches out from your shoulders, with your fingers pointing forwards. Keeping your body straight, exhale and push up, arms straight. Think strength into your abdomen, chest and arms as you go. Inhaling, bend your arms and lower your body as low as you can while still keeping it straight, and exhaling, push up again. Continue for your maximum. When you feel you are finished think strong and go for just one more. It is useful to rest in the praying stretch afterwards.

Many women and some men find the press-ups are an intimidating exercise because of its macho image, and because it *does* require strength to do. I know that I watch in dismay when people in the gym or the *dojang* effortlessly rattle off dozens of press-ups when I am trembling with effort. Nevertheless, once you have the strength to perform press-ups correctly, a beneficent circle is created where performing them will quickly make you more strong. Sometimes do them rapidly, and sometimes slowly and smoothly. Forget the mystique and do press-ups for your own sake to develop your own strength.

Add full press-ups into your toning session during Weeks One, Two and Three of Project Three.

LEG EXTENSION SIT-UPS

Even the most resilient abdominal muscles need new challenges to keep them in good shape. It is always useful to have more and tougher variations up your sleeve to stop you from becoming lax and bored. Try out this one.

- Lying flat on your back, reach straight up with your right leg and extend your left leg out parallel to the floor, toes pointed. Lace your hands behind your head and bring your forearms alongside your face. Exhaling, lift your upper body towards your right leg, inhaling, come part of the way down. Lift and lower 8 times, then change legs and lift and lower another 8 times. Then do 8 sit-ups with both legs straight up. Keep your abdomen flexed in towards your spine throughout. When you are finished, hug your knees in towards your chest, and relax your lower back.

Fit this sit-up variation into your toning session during Weeks Four, Five and Six.

LEG EXTENSIONS

- Stand tall, with your feet together. Lift your abdomen, tuck your tailbone under. Lift the crown of your head, lengthen the back of your neck, and relax your shoulders. Stretch your arms out to the side shoulder height.
- Lift your right knee as you inhale. As you exhale, stretch your right leg straight out in front of you. Point your toes. Hold for a count of 5, breathing steadily, then bend the knee to bring the leg in. Finish by putting your foot back on the floor. Do the same with the left leg.
- Repeat three more times each side.

This is an extraordinarily demanding exercise, although it looks easy! Do what you can with the lifted leg; you are trying to get it at least parallel to the floor. Trained dancers and yoga practitioners can fluently bring the lifted foot to eye level.

Be particularly careful not to screw your face up with effort; keep your eyes and throat soft.

Fit leg extensions into your toning time during Weeks Seven, Eight and Nine of Project Three.

LEG LIFTS AND LOCUSTS

These two toning exercises are of interest to you if you are, as one woman described herself, 'starting to face up to my bottom'. They both tone the bottom rather well and you can feel a lifting and tightening pretty soon after you start to do them.

LEG LIFTS

- Start on all fours, knees hip-distance apart and hands shoulder-distance apart. Lengthen the back of your neck.
- Lift your abdominal muscles, straighten your right leg out behind you, toes touching the floor. Exhaling, lift it, and, inhaling, lower almost to the floor but not quite. Do 15 reps up and down, moving smoothly and slowly. Do not just throw the leg, really feel the muscles work.
- Now change, and do 15 on the left, just as carefully, just as attentively.
- Come back to all fours, sit back on your heels, and stretch forwards along your thighs, arms in front of you on the floor in praying stretch.

THE LOCUST

- Lie on the floor on your abdomen, knees and feet together, arms alongside your body and palms down. On an exhalation, lift your knees and feet, and lift your head, chest and arms in a beautiful aerodynamic shape. Breathe steadily and hold for 5 counts, then, exhaling, sink gently to the ground. Repeat 2 more times, then push up onto all fours and back into praying stretch again.

Try to get leg lifts and locusts fitted into your toning time during Weeks Ten, Eleven and Twelve of this Project, and indeed at any other time when you are feeling interested in the shape of your bottom!

Stress management and relaxation

These skills are just as important as the dynamic physical ones. Do not lose track of them during Project Three. Here are some new techniques for you to try. They are all doors into the same room, the room being simply a sense of peace. However, if you know about lots of doors, if one will not open, there are several others you could try.

Tratak

Tratak, or steady gazing, is an excellent concentration exercise. By helping you to concentrate it helps to clear the worries away from your mind. Try it out in your stress management times during Weeks One and Two. Tratak is simple to describe, though because of our Western mental restlessness it can be hard to perform.

- Choose something on which to focus your gaze; it could be a candle flame, a shell or a stone you like, a crystal, a flower, anything you feel like looking at. Sit yourself down, cross legged if possible, and put your object in a position where you can look at it easily.

- Now, check your posture, lifting and light, and alternately gaze at your object for a little while, then close your eyes and visualize it with your eyes closed. When its image fades from your mind, open your eyes again and look at the object for a while. Carry on alternating opening and closing your eyes as long as feels right for you. If your mind wanders, just keep bringing your attention back to the object. When you want to stop, simply close your eyes and relax. Take a moment or two to become aware of the room around you, then blink your eyes open to let in the light.

- Do not rush. Have a moment or two to collect your thoughts before you move on to the other activities of the day.

The safe place

'The safe place' is a guided fantasy which you can use very quickly if you need to. It is a sort of emotional first aid.

The first part of it is to find the safe place, and work out what it is like for you.

Either in savasana, *or sitting cross-legged on the floor, relax, breathe steadily and let the worries and anxieties of the day drain away from you. Just let them flow away. . . .*

Now take yourself in your imagination to a place where you would really like to be. Allow it to be whatever comes – the first place that comes into your mind. It could be a warm and sunny beach, or a firelit room, a cool snowy landscape, a mountainside looking over a huge panorama. Choose the place that comes into your mind. . . .

Take your time noticing everything about your place: the sights, the shapes, the colours, the textures, the fragrances and the sounds. Have a good look around and really observe everything. When you have absorbed everything about your place, return your awareness to the room you are in, the here and now. Yawn and stretch to awaken the body, and blink your eyes open to let in the light. . . .

You have identified your safe place; the next step is to visualize a quick way to it. It is useful to practise like this. You want to be able to spend 2 minutes, or 5 minutes, in your safe place when you are in the middle of a fraught day, because to do so will 'ground', relax and restore you. Think of where you are now – sitting at your desk, struggling on the bus or tube, whatever. Imagine yourself stepping into a lift. The doors close and the light over the doors tells you that you are on the tenth floor. Press the button for first floor. Feel the lift go down and watch the numbers changing: 9, 8, 7, 6, all the way down to 1. At the first floor the doors open and you step out – straight into your safe place. See yourself sit or lie down in your safe place and soak up everything about it which you love, everything that is special for you. . . .

When it is time, step back into the lift with a lighter heart and a stronger spirit, and go back up to the tenth floor, the here and now.

With practice you can visit your safe place briefly but with enormously beneficent effect, whenever it is useful to you to do so.

The safe place itself will change from time to time. If it ever becomes stale, imagine yourself a fresh one.

Use this as an alternative to alcohol and tranquillizers as an instantly accessible response to anxiety.

(A quick common-sense point: of course do *not* do this visualization while you are driving or operating machinery or supervising activities. It is a few moments snatched from the day and turned into something useful, but you have to be free of responsibility for your own or anybody else's safety during those moments.)

Become skilled at transporting yourself swiftly to a safe place during Weeks Three and Four of Project Three.

Speaking partner

Here is a practical stress management skill: finding and developing a relationship with a Speaking Partner. It is common enough for there to be 'nobody to talk to' at work. Because you have to be strategic, it may be impossible to be open in the workplace. It may be difficult to talk over work issues with a partner at home, however loving, who does not work in the same field as you do.

An objective you can set yourself in Weeks Five and Six is to identify a person who might be a good Speaking Partner for you. Ideally it should be somebody in a similar field to yours, but not in the same organization. It should be someone with whom you are unlikely to come into competition for future jobs, and, finally, someone who also wants a good understanding 'ear' to whom they can talk about issues arising at work. Set yourselves up to speak with agreed frequency (once a week, once a month?) for an agreed length of time each (20 minutes, half-an-hour?) and to provide each other with good, supportive listening, either on the phone or by getting together.

This is different from a gossip or a chat, or giving and receiving advice. It is an exchange of good, active listening, honest feedback if requested, and a space to reflect, in friendly company, on what is going on for you.

My Speaking Partner is a key person in my life. I can store up triumphs, disasters and puzzles to share with her. I can sound off about things when I need to, ask for advice or feedback when I need it, or work things through with a well-informed and empathetic interlocutor; and I provide the same things for her. We have a bond of confidentiality between the two of us, agreed at the outset and long proved reliable.

By providing yourself with somebody like this, you both take a positive step to alleviate stress in your life and give them an opportunity to do the same in theirs.

Meditation

You have already tried out the foundation skill of meditation in the previous Project, when you worked on 'Clearing the Mind'. In Weeks Seven and Eight book three 20-minute slots per week in your diary and use them for this.

- Sit on the floor, cross-legged if you can. Lift your abdomen and relax your hips. Lift your spine and the crown of your head, lengthen the back of your neck and relax your shoulders. Let your eyes close and let your breathing steady. Instruct your mind to be silent and forget all thoughts of past, present, and future. Do not attempt to control the restlessness of your mind, as this will only agitate it further. Just detach yourself from your thoughts and let them go. They will become fewer and fewer. At times they may cease. If they do, even for a while, you will have the experience which Zen buddhists call 'empty and marvellous'.

It is often explained like this. When the surface of a lake is rippled and ruffled, all you can see is the water's surface. If the ripples stop and the surface becomes smooth, you can see all the way down to the bottom. That is how our minds are. The constant passage of thoughts ripple the surface of the mind. If we can cause the thoughts to stop, if only for a while, then the water is clear and we can see all the way down to the bottom, to our true selves.

Meditation cannot really be taught, learned or forced. You make time for it and do these one or two simple things, and at some point it happens spontaneously. You may be delighted to find how simple and non-esoteric meditation is. Its stress-relieving effect is in its immediate creation of quiet calm time, and in its long-term capacity to shift one's perspective about what matters and what does not. Meditation will not turn you into a fey, passive dreamer, but it may stop you worrying about things you always knew were not worth worrying about anyway.

Chanting

Even if you see yourself as a pragmatic industrialist or a systematic professional, you may have found yourself able to take on the idea that meditation might be useful to you relatively easily, but you may draw the line at chanting. Oh no, you may think, not me, definitely not.

Think how many unexpected things you have done since the beginning of Project One, and how very useful many of them have been to you. See if you can suspend your disbelief for a while about chanting: it really might be a revelation!

Book yourself six 10-minute sessions for chanting in Weeks Nine and Ten and use these as times to play with and get to know the sounds your voice makes and the different vibrations it makes in different parts of your body.

The good effects you will get are these:

- your voice will become deeper and more mellifluous;
- you will be able to speak both more expressively and more authoritatively because you are more 'in touch' with your voice;
- you will find a sense of calm spread right through you as you practice, which remains with you for some time afterwards.

- Sit as for meditation.

- On the outbreaths, try out these sounds with your voice:
  mm
  ee
  ooh
  oh
  ah

- Let the sounds last the same length of time as the breath.

- Do several of each and notice where they seem to vibrate: lips? forehead? chest? hips? Where do you chiefly *feel* the sound happening? First experience the sounds as physical events.

Spend a couple of sessions doing that, and you will already be exploring and developing your voice.

You can take this further into chanting *mantram* if you wish to. A *mantra* is a seed-sound from Sanskrit. Sound is a form of energy, and some kinds of energy are healing or inspiring – a *mantra* has those qualities. Use the ancient seed-sound 'ohm'. Divide it into:

'Oh' felt deep in the hips
'Oo' moving up through the thorax into the throat and mouth
'mm' in the lips

Make the whole sound the same length as the breath, and make the part of the *mantra* where your mouth is open last the same length of time as the part where it is closed. Do not gasp in between chants: just breathe in gently. Pitch the sound wherever it comes spontaneously. Go on for a while and then stop: that is all. Take your time. Reflect gently within on what you are doing and how it feels.

There are many *mantram* but it is better if they are passed to you by a guru, and I am sure that if that is what is meant to happen in your life, you will come across somebody who can do this for you, however unlikely it seems. There are also many exciting voice and chant workshops. You may like to follow up on these if getting into your voice is giving you a great deal of joy; or you may feel you would like to join a choir.

In Weeks Eleven and Twelve choose any stress management and relaxation activities you have enjoyed, and use them in your Stress Management times. Simply remember to do a specific focused activity in this area at least three times a week.

Lifestyle

In this Project we will work on ideas in the Lifestyle section which push both your self-awareness and your inner resources a little further.

Anthology

Most of us from time to time come across phrases in songs, snatches of poems, words in films, sudden insights in novels or plays, which catch our emotions, express something we have long wished to express, or simply seem beautiful. Life rushes on and the words get lost.

Buy a notebook and make it your anthology – whenever you come across an arresting insight or a moving description, copy it into your notebook, and thus make your own very personal collection. It will accrue slowly, a little at a time, and will be a great resource for you.

The lifestyle slot for two weeks is devoted to getting this started: all that really means is to organize yourself a book and build an awareness into your life that you will record material that you find apposite or moving.

After that, it will take care of itself and simply grow. As with all the Lifestyle positive actions, the aim is to create an activity which is not an 'artificial' thing to do, but a natural and ordinary part of life.

Dream diary

365 nights of the year we perform the supremely creative act of dreaming. Often we are not aware of it: our dreams take care of themselves. In dramatic or troubled parts of our lives our dreams become vivid and we do remember them, and occasionally a blissful dream remains in our minds, enhancing the following day with a glow of pleasure.

You might like to get more in touch with your dreams. Freud called dreams 'the royal road to the unconscious mind', and certainly increasing our sensitivity to dreams can increase our sense of what is going on in our unconscious minds.

Keep a notebook and pen by your bed. If a dream wakes you in the night, make some notes describing it in your book. In the mornings, as soon as you wake, make brief notes on your dreams. You have to do this instantly on waking because dreams evaporate so rapidly as the conscious and logical part of the day begins.

What do you do with this knowledge of your dreams? 'Dream dictionaries' which give 'this-equals-that' equations for the meaning of dreams omit the unique personal history and content of your own life, your own iconography. A creative way to respond is simply to be watchful and intuitive about your dreams, and let them speak to you. You will gain all kinds of insights about your own qualities and desires just by letting your dreams rest in your mind and seeing what they have to say to you.

During Weeks Three and Four keep a dream diary and see what happens for you if you give some attention to the dreaming part of yourself.

The Way of the Warrior

> *'For Chinese thinkers however, the basic question is not "What is the Truth?" but "Where is the Way?"'* (A. C. Graham, Introduction to Lieh Tzu)

The Lifestyle idea to consider in Weeks Five and Six is taking up a martial art. If your reaction is, as it might have been about chanting (p. 94), 'Oh no, definitely not, not me', just pause for a moment and suspend your disbelief.

Life is a struggle, we know that. Coping with all the contradictions inside ourselves is a struggle too. We fight battles within and without, all the time.

The martial arts are not fighting sports, they are 'Ways'. The 'Do' in their names means 'Way': Judo, the gentle way; Karate Do, the way of the empty hand; Tae Kwon Do, the way of the foot and the fist; Aikido, the way of spirit combat. 'Way' means 'way of life' or 'spiritual path'.

If you study a martial art you will become fit and strong and learn some useful self-defence; but if you stick with it you will gain much more than that. The real battle, you soon find, is the struggle inside. The kind of courage you develop, as you will feel in the presence of a true martial artist, is very quiet, very gentle, very subtle.

If the overt athleticism of some styles puts you off, consider the 'soft' or 'internal' arts such as Tai Chi or Aikido which are less obviously demanding in their initial stages – although if you persevere with them they will make you every bit as powerful as the 'hard' or 'external' arts (Karate, Tae Kwon Do, etc.).

The crucial thing in choosing a class is the attitude of the instructor and the atmosphere which he or she creates. Go and watch a few classes in different styles in your area. In a good class the atmosphere will be calm, cheerful, and very focused and concentrated. The instructor's own technique will be very focused and accurate, but he or she will be concentrating on enabling class members rather than showing off his or her own technique. There will be high standards maintained without gratuitously destructive feedback going on. Be aware of how any women in the class are treated and be clear that you feel comfortable with this, whether you are male or female yourself.

By going and looking at two or three classes you will probably find one which you are particularly drawn to, and that will probably be the one which is right for you.

This is *not* compulsory: but I do feel very strongly that many of us in the West can be greatly enriched and helped by learning one of the martial arts of the East. Give it some good thought in Weeks Five and Six.

> *'Karate-do is attained a step at a time, and so is life. Just train every day and try your best, and the truth will come to you.'* (Ken Singleton, *An Introduction to Karate*)

Positive visioning

Try some positive visioning in Weeks Seven and Eight.

- Take 5 minutes to brainstorm (i.e. to write quickly, without self-censoring or inhibition) all the things you would like to achieve at work during the next 2 years. Review your list and circle every item which is either clearly realistically possible or means a great deal to you. Now write a paragraph describing yourself doing all the circled items. Be positive and clear. Don't worry about how strange it feels – just do it. Notice what it is like to think of yourself and describe yourself in such a positive manner. Does it make these aims seem more feasible? Is it a relief to acknowledge what your aims and ambitions are? What other thoughts and feelings cross your mind as you reflect on these issues?

- Now, continuing to take your intentions calmly and

seriously, write for each item at least *one* action point, and next to each action point write a time target.

This visioning exercise is not a question of indulging in fairytale fantasy, but of not getting blocked by negative feelings and unnecessary self-doubt. Whenever you need to form a positive vision, use the framework – imagination, selection and planning – to plug your energies into where they need to be.

Try it first in the form you have it in above. At other times substitute:

– 'all the things you would like to achieve regarding your health and fitness';

– 'all the things you would like to achieve creatively';

– 'all the things you would like to work out in your family life'.

as the defining phrase.

Use this technique whenever you need it, and use Weeks Seven and Eight of Project Three to become familiar with it.

For the final month of Project Three repeat any of the Lifestyle exercises from any of the Projects that you found particularly useful, or feel as though you would like to use again.

PROJECT 3

Cardio	Flexibility	Toning	Relaxation	Comment

WEEK 1

Cardio	Flexibility	Toning	Relaxation
3 × 30 mins or attend club or class ☐ ☐ ☐ ? pyramids ☐	3 × 30 mins ☐ ☐ ☐ or class ☐ learn 'Salute to the Sun' ☐	3 × 20 mins ☐ ☐ ☐ or attend club or class ☐ try full press ups (p. 88) ☐	Try Tratak (p. 91) ☐ ☐ ☐

WEEK 2

Cardio	Flexibility	Toning	Relaxation
3 × 30 mins or attend club or class ☐ ☐ ☐ ? pyramids ☐	3 × 30 mins ☐ ☐ ☐ or class ☐ 'Salute to the Sun' ☐	3 × 20 mins ☐ ☐ ☐ or attend club or class ☐ full press ups ☐	Tratak ☐ ☐ ☐

WEEK 3

Cardio	Flexibility	Toning	Relaxation
3 × 30 mins or attend club or class ☐ ☐ ☐ ? pyramids ☐	3 × 30 mins ☐ ☐ ☐ or class ☐ 'Salute to the Sun' ☐	3 × 20 mins ☐ ☐ ☐ or attend club or class ☐ full press ups ☐	Tratak ☐

102 Fit To Work

Cardio	Flexibility	Toning	Relaxation	Comment

WEEK 4

| 3 × 30 mins ☐ ☐ ☐ ? Fartlek ☐ | 3 × 30 mins ☐ ☐ ☐ or class ☐ learn leg stretches (p. 84) ☐ | 3 × 20 mins ☐ ☐ ☐ or attend club or class ☐ leg extension sit-ups (p. 88) ☐ | The 'Safe Place' (p. 91) ☐ ☐ ☐ | |

WEEK 5

| 3 × 30 mins ☐ ☐ ☐ ? Fartlek ☐ | 3 × 30 mins ☐ ☐ ☐ or class ☐ leg stretches ☐ | 3 × 20 mins ☐ ☐ ☐ or attend club or class ☐ leg extension sit-ups (p. 88) ☐ | The 'Safe Place' ☐ ☐ ☐ | |

WEEK 6

| 3 × 30 mins ☐ ☐ ☐ ? Fartlek ☐ | 3 × 30 mins ☐ ☐ ☐ or class ☐ leg stretches ☐ | 3 × 20 mins ☐ ☐ ☐ or attend class or club ☐ leg extension sit-ups ☐ | Find a 'Speaking Partner' (p. 93) ☐ | |

Cardio	Flexibility	Toning	Relaxation	Comment

WEEK 7

3 × 30 mins
☐ ☐ ☐

? new route or style
☐

3 × 30 mins
☐ ☐ ☐

more back bends (p. 85)
☐

3 × 20 mins
☐ ☐ ☐

or club or class
☐

leg extensions (p. 89)
☐

Begin to meditate (p. 94)
☐ ☐ ☐

WEEK 8

3 × 30 mins
☐ ☐ ☐

? new route or style
☐

3 × 30 mins
☐ ☐ ☐

more back bends
☐

3 × 20 mins
☐ ☐ ☐

or club or class
☐

leg extensions
☐

Begin to meditate
☐ ☐ ☐

WEEK 9

3 × 30 mins
☐ ☐ ☐

? new route or style
☐

3 × 30 mins
☐ ☐ ☐

more back bends
☐

3 × 20 mins
☐ ☐ ☐

or club or class
☐

leg extensions
☐

Try chanting (p. 94)
☐ ☐ ☐

104 Fit To Work

Cardio	Flexibility	Toning	Relaxation	Comment

WEEK 10

| 3 × 30 mins ☐ ☐ ☐ | 3 × 30 mins ☐ ☐ ☐ | 3 × 20 mins ☐ ☐ ☐ | Try chanting ☐ ☐ ☐ | |
| ? circuits ☐ | try 'spectacular stretches' (p. 86) ☐ | or club or class ☐

leg lifts and locusts (p. 89) ☐ | | |

WEEK 11

| 3 × 30 mins ☐ ☐ ☐ | 3 × 30 mins ☐ ☐ ☐ | 3 × 20 mins ☐ ☐ ☐ | Stress management (your own choice) ☐ ☐ ☐ | |
| ? circuits ☐ | 'spectacular stretches' ☐ | or club or class ☐

leg lifts and locusts ☐ | | |

WEEK 12

| 3 × 30 mins ☐ ☐ ☐ | 3 × 30 mins ☐ ☐ ☐ | 3 × 20 mins ☐ ☐ ☐ | Stress management (your own choice) ☐ ☐ ☐ | |
| ? circuits ☐ | 'spectacular stretches' ☐ | or club or class ☐

leg lifts and locusts ☐ | | |

PROJECT 3: LIFESTYLE

WEEKS 1 & 2: *Start an anthology* ☐

WEEKS 3 & 4: *Write a dream diary* ☐

WEEKS 5 & 6: *Consider a martial art?* ☐

WEEKS 7 & 8: *Begin Positive Visioning* ☐

WEEKS 9–12: *Concentrate on any of the above you find fruitful* ☐ ☐ ☐ ☐

Notes: ....

Project Four

There are several different ways in which pressure can hit us during our careers, and all of them have an impact on our health, fitness, emotional state and ability to take care of ourselves. The aim of the Project is to provide some ideas as to how to tackle those pressures. If I have heard people say 'I am too tired to exercise' or 'I am too tense to exercise' once, I have heard it a thousand times, and yet if you can get over that hurdle and do something, something *appropriate* for your current situation, then you feel so much better, infinitely better than if you try to knock the tension or sluggishness on the head with alcohol or an overload of rich food.

The key word is of course *appropriate*. If you have always run seven and a half miles a week and now you are pregnant and suddenly have to commute one and a half hours a day to and from a new job, running seven and a half miles a week is probably *not* appropriate. Conversely, if you have always worked outdoors and on your feet, and regarded a yoga class and a sauna quite enough exercise for the week, you need to rethink if you are moved to a sedentary indoor desk job. Working out what is appropriate at any particular phase of your life is reliant on three things:

1   common sense;
2   some basic insights into fitness;
3   knowing your own body and not being passive about it.

Let us assume that the common sense is there and that some basic information about fitness has been put in place by the book.

The third part of this is perhaps more difficult. We feel passive about our bodies because we feel that other people are the 'experts': sports scientists, doctors, physiotherapists, whatever.

We wait for somebody to tell us what we ought to be doing, or thinking, or feeling. We need confirmation from an 'expert' that we are training 'hard' enough, or that we are at the 'correct' weight.

Specialized information and advice from experts *is* of course invaluable. But we need to balance this with a very clear conception of taking responsibility for ourselves.

Nobody knows better than you do whether you are well or ill. Nobody knows better than you do whether you are tired or fresh. The trouble is that that knowledge may have been obscured under layers of negative conditioning. It may have been fouled up in just the same way many women's clear self-knowledge about hunger, food and eating has been fouled up, that is, by contrary cultural messages.

When you do a demanding exercise, there comes a point where you want to stop. If you want to get fitter, you have to carry on just a bit longer, push into that boundary just a bit more.

But, if the 'carry on even though it hurts' message has got at all tangled up with your emotions about being a worthwhile person, or being weak or strong, or being a failure or a success, you will find it hard to know how long is long enough to push into that pain. It turns from a straightforward question into a complicated one, just as for most women the question 'Do you feel like something to eat?' has turned from a straightforward question into a complicated one over the last twenty years.

We have to start stripping those layers of complication away to be really fit and well. We have to learn to validate our sense of tiredness when we are tired, to validate and overcome our sense of sluggishness when we are lethargic, and to celebrate our sense of strength and fitness when we are well. Whatever choice you make about exercising or not exercising on any particular day, validate it and yourself, and then relax, accept and celebrate your choice, and think no more about it.

In terms of quantity and intensity of exercise, think all the time about balance. Assess the physical and emotional demands your job and your private life are making on you and design your programme accordingly. Breast-feeding a baby three times a night and holding down a job-share is not the moment to take up hang-gliding or start training for a marathon, but some fresh-air walking and some gentle yoga or swimming will be ideal. A job which keeps you tied to a desk and a quiet undemanding home life, or a work or a home situation where you cope with a lot of pent-up emotion, may create a need for an exercise programme where you do plenty of vigorous activity, get up a good sweat and lose some adrenaline.

At special times, such as when you are travelling and disrupted because of that, or going through a health crisis or an emotional crisis, be flexible and creative and adjust your programme, rather than bashing away regardless or giving up altogether.

Let us look at some special circumstances and the exercises both physical and mental which may be useful.

Travelling

Jet lag

If you travel across time zones you may experience jet lag, but its detrimental effects *can* be minimized. Use this checklist.

- Start in the mind: decide that you are not going to let jet lag be a big deal.

- As soon as it is clear that the plane is in the air and not going to turn back, change your watch to the time zone you are going to. As far as possible, eat and drink according to that time zone straight away.

- Do not drink more than a couple of units of alcohol on the flight. Have plenty of water.

- On day flights, do not work the whole time on the flight. Do some work by all means, but intersperse it with spells of light reading and daydreaming.

- On night flights, sleep if you can, do some breathing and relaxation exercises if you cannot. Do not panic: your body will take up the extra sleep it needs later. Yoga students are the envy of other passengers on long-haul flights as they slip easily from *savasana* into sleep.

- When you arrive, try to stay up until at least 9 p.m. bedtime in your new time zone. If you wake at 2 a.m. that night, again, do not panic: breathe, relax. You will get the sleep you need over the next few days. If you cannot sleep, accept it and just rest.

You may well find the exercises from 'Overland Journeys' and 'Total Exhaustion' useful after flying too.

Overland journeys

Whether you are making long trips by train or by car the extraordinarily awful design of the seats may well mean your back is aching by the time you arrive. This may be the case after flying as well.

Go all the way back to Project One, Basic Stretching (p. 17). Do this sequence after you have checked in wherever you are going. It only takes 15 minutes. It is well worth it, to ease out all the cramps and stiffnesses before they turn into really troublesome aches and pains or indeed actually start to distort your body.

In addition, try the following exercises.

HAND EXERCISES

If you have gripped a steering wheel for several hundred miles, your hands may well feel quite stressed and stiff.

- With your right hand, bend each finger of your left hand back as far as it will go, one at a time. Bend the thumb back, and then down towards your wrist too. Do the same thing with the left hand, to the right. Now, with your right hand, grasp each finger low down and pull firmly along it. Do the thumb as well, then change over. Finally, shake your wrists up and down half a dozen times, side to side half a dozen times, circle six times in one direction, and six times the other way.

Now your hands feel a bit more human again!

RELAXATION

Some people love to travel. Many more of us are scared of planes, scared of terrorists, worried we have lost the tickets, lost the way and will never get home again. This stress is not stupid or naïve, or paranoid: it is *normal*.

You may not have the time or inclination for a long elaborate relaxation. Have a quick one instead.

- Snatch a moment to close your eyes and imagine you are floating on your back in a warm blue lagoon. Above you the sky is blue, the sun is shining. You are soaking up the warmth of the sun. A warm breeze is ruffling the palm trees at the water's edge and flickering over your body. The only sound is the water's gentle lapping.

Just a few seconds of that can bring your blood pressure down and your humanity and sense of humour back into the frame. Use it!

Total exhaustion

I invented these exercises when I fell whimpering with exhaustion into a hotel bed, 'too tired to sleep' because my body was all messed up by sedentary travelling. Use them when you are in the same boat.

Lying in bed,

- flex and point your feet slowly 6 times.
- circle your feet at the ankles slowly, 6 times in one direction, 6 times the other.
- put the soles of your feet together and pull them up as close as you can to the perineum. Flop your knees out to the side. Hold the stretch, breathing steadily, for a slow count of 10.
- stretch both arms over to the right, shoulder level, and look over to the right. Flop both knees, still bent, over to the left. Breathe steadily and hold for 10.

- reverse it, arms to the left, knees bent and flopped over to the right. Look left. Breathe steadily and hold for 10.
- stretch your legs out straight again. Lace your fingers together and push your palms straight up towards the ceiling, arms straight. Breathe steadily and hold for 5. Float your arms down.
- lace your fingers together and push your palms straight up over your head, arms straight. Mind the headboard! Breathe steadily and hold for 5, then float your arms down.
- settle your arms by your sides, and bend your knees up, feet flat on the bed. Exhale and flex your abdomen into your spine and curl your pubic bone up as if aiming it towards your navel. Inhale and release. Repeat 6 times.
- same position, squeeze and release your buttock muscles. Repeat 6 times.
- stretch out, yawn and relax.
- sleep!

Outsides and insides

Planes, trains, and automobiles are all dehydrating environments. Minimize the discomfort of this by taking with you plenty of whatever skin care products you care for: essentially a toner and moisturizer and a body lotion. It is no longer naff or suspect for men to do this: it is just common sense.

Dehydration and a change of diet can quickly constipate you. It is horrible trying to transact business and relate to clients when distracted by an uncomfortable gut. Watch your diet *before* you go away and make sure you are eating plenty of fresh fruit and vegetables and drinking plenty of fluids. While you are away drink plenty of water and fruit juices and when choosing food keep a good intake of fibre up. In this way you will avoid this irritating side-effect of travel!

High anxiety

We can undergo high anxiety because things are going spectacularly badly at work or at home, and it can also happen when things are going spectacularly well and a creative overflow is disturbing our rhythms.

Positive crisis

Over-excitement because things are going so well or developing so fast can be 'treated' in terms of fitness, by a combination of things.

1. Increase your cardiovascular training a little. Not a huge amount, just a manageable addition. If you normally do a 15-minute run, make it 20 for the time being; or if you go to one dance or aerobic class per week, make it 2 for a bit. Burning up more of the adrenaline you are producing will help you to continue sleeping well even though you are high.

2. Good breathing is important too. Short, shallow breathing high up in the chest is a characteristic of excitement. Return to basic abdominal breathing (p. 35) and alternate nostril breathing (p. 63) at some point every day. It will slow down your racing mind.

3. Lastly, if you have enjoyed the explorations in the Lifestyle part of the Projects, your philosophical base may have shifted somewhat. It is genuinely useful, at those rare and precious times when it is success rather than failure that seems to be running away with you, to have a clear perspective about your own values and what really matters to you.

Negative crisis

What tends to happen physically if things are going particularly badly at work? If you are *angry*, and you have made weight training part of your toning programme, I very much recommend that you go to the gym and pump some iron! Do not let your rage fool you into injuring yourself, but enjoy the fact that you will get through your sets far more easily than usual, powered by your anger. Emphasize the stretching part of your programme because distress and depression often cause us to collapse the soft front surface of the body. Stretch the front of the body and the spine regularly, literally to 'open your heart'. The gentle, unpunishing but satisfying nature of stretching is a good antidote to conflict and disruption at work.

Bad results and bad atmospheres at work can interfere with your sleep too. Use any of the relaxation techniques which you can connect with and also be aware that sometimes the most constructive strategy is to accept that you cannot sleep but you can relax and release your muscles and rest.

Use visualizations such as picturing a large box at the bottom of the stairs with a heavy lid. Into the box drop all your concerns about work. Shut the heavy lid, and be clear that the problems will stay in the box until the next morning when you open the lid again.

The work you have done on exploring yourself and your values in the Lifestyle section of the Projects may help. If your job is tearing you apart, give yourself some time and space to think about why and to work your survival strategy out – maybe your exit strategy too. Value yourself enough to make the changes you need to and to take care of yourself through hard times which you cannot alter or avoid.

Negative crises can be personal as well as work-related, and personal crises can impact severely on both your work and your health. Marital break-up, illness or worryingly bad behaviour in children, the death of parents, financial difficulties, can crop up in any combination (and often in a grand slam appalling all-in-one-go) at exactly the point when your career is also at its most challenging and your body beginning to give you messages about the approach of middle age.

Very bad shocks like bereavement or the break-up of a marriage knock the stuffing out of you physically and may necessitate a period of leave from work if that is possible in your field. They are also sometimes strangely liberating, since they seem to knock most of the difficulties of life into a perspective where they seem very trivial. A light-headed sense that nothing much matters sometimes accompanies periods of acute personal pain.

Numbness, exhaustion and preoccupation will preclude complicated and fussy exercise régimes. Make sure you eat; probably little and often is all you will be able to face, but have milk and fruit and bread and cheese to keep you going. The weight loss experienced at such times (although usually welcome to women because of our ludicrous culturally-imposed obsession with thinness) is a result of shock and shows that your body is burning its emergency stores fast, and you must respect the need to replenish them. Failing to eat on top of everything else which is happening will make your brain chemistry even more haywire and erratic – do not impose that extra burden on yourself.

As for exercise, walk. Walking has a gentle natural rhythm which helps to unravel emotions and think through shock and grief. It gets you out of the rooms where dreadful things happened and were said and it reconnects you with trees, sky, birds, plants and stones in a helpful way. It helps your body systems to keep strong and see you through.

Pregnancy and parenthood

This generation of professional women and men are, some of them at least, engaged in negotiations for flexible packages of employment around pregnancy and early parenthood. I hope the next decade will see the back of the terrible spectacle of women being encouraged to carry on 'as normal' while pregnant and get 'back to normal' and back to their desks within days of giving birth as though they had had a bout of flu rather than produced a new human being. This phase was a necessary one to go through in order to give the lie to the 'woman can't cope' myth, but it is not humane to mothers, fathers or babies. Extensive and flexible parental leave, supported alternative child care and imaginative work patterns *are* developing which should enable parents and children, eventually, to have a happier time.

If you are pregnant, take plenty of rest and keep doing your stretching exercises (excepting back bends where you lie on your tummy on the floor). Do not do strenuous toning exercises and do not take up any new cardiovascular activities. Some women who are already well-conditioned runners continue to run well into their pregnancies, but only do this if you are already very fit. Always tell the instructor of any class you attend that you are pregnant.

Breathing well and relaxation skills are important during pregnancy and birth, so make time for these.

When the baby is born, both parents need to regard themselves as birthing people for at least four months. That means taking care of yourselves and each other as well as the baby, and *that* means taking care of the basics like rest and food, giving each other time to talk and listen about how you are finding family life without feeling obliged to say it is all wonderful, and it means giving each other small pieces of time (start with half an hour each twice a week) where one parent cares for the baby while the other does some exercise.

In this part of your life, choose whatever kind of exercise you *really* feel like, and find what comes easily. This is not the moment for stern challenges, but it *is* the moment to give some time to looking after your own body as well as looking after the baby's.

If you are a woman who has just given birth, you may have deflated neatly back into your pre-pregnancy clothes – but you may not! I never did. Do not panic at the astonishing softness of your abdomen, hugeness of your breasts, and thickening of waist, upper arms and thighs. Your body will do a fantastic job of healing and re-strengthening. You can help it, *not* by crash-dieting, but by having a balanced diet which emphasizes fresh fruits, vegetables, and nuts, pulses, and wholemeal breads and grains; and *not* by engaging in a frantic exercise programme, but by going right back to Project One stretching and toning, and only when you feel up to it (two weeks after delivery at the earliest) the Project One cardiovascular programme. Visualize being back into your old clothes within six months rather than six weeks: then if it is sooner that is a bonus. Have a few intermediate outfits to see you through.

As parents of a tiny baby, sleep is a priority if you do not have one of the rare babies who gives up night feeds after a month or two. Be intelligent and flexible about sleeping arrangements so you both get enough sleep to cope. If you have a loving physical relationship which is important to you, do not let your baby destroy your sex life. Babies have terrific anti-sex radar and often cry just as you are beginning to remind yourselves of the basic moves. Make love at different times of the day and in different bits of the house if just after you get into bed at night is regularly sabotaged by your offspring.

Redundancy

There used to be many professions and degrees of seniority within organizations where you simply never lost your job unless you committed a sizeable misdemeanour. These days it can happen to anyone.

The crisis of self-esteem which accompanies being made redundant can hardly be over-estimated, particularly for those of us who trained and built our careers up on the basis that if you did all the right things you could expect to be employed for the rest of your life.

I believe that fitness can be more than a useful adjunct if a redundancy is part of your working life: it can be a life-saver. Prioritize your exercise programme and use some of your extra time to develop it further. If you have a gym membership, keep it going if you can afford to, but if you have to let it go, accept the fact and work a coherent programme out for yourself using the things you can do without a gym – jogging or running, stretching and the type of toning exercises we have had in the Projects where you are using parts of your own body weight for resistance work. Use the breathing and relaxation techniques you have developed to cope with the inevitable mood swings and periods of doubt that will hit you.

Your job can be moved, but nobody can take your body away from you, and deepening your self knowledge while growing fitter and stronger will have a fundamental role in keeping you sane and clear about your own value. If and when those terrifying elusive interviews for a new job do come, you will look and feel so much better when you attend, through your hard work on the physical *and* the relaxation disciplines in this book.

Afterword

If you have followed through and worked on the Projects in *Fit to Work* I hope you have enjoyed yourself and experienced real benefits, both at work and away from it, from a more 'live' relationship with your body *and* your feelings. Congratulate yourself on having the stamina and imagination to motivate yourself along that road.

If you have dipped into the book and pulled out odd exercises and odd ideas that have been useful for particular circumstances that is terrific too.

No exercise system, however holistic (which is certainly what this one has aimed to be), is a panacea, but I am deeply committed to the conviction that *everybody* can feel better and work better if they are prepared to give even a moderate amount of attention to the body which they live in. So I hope that this book has provoked and inspired some sense of that connection for you.

Further Reading

Eknath Easwaran (ed.), *The Bhagavad-Gita*. Arkana 1986.
John Heider, *The Tao of Leadership*. Wildwood House 1986.
B. K. S. Iyengar, *Light on Pranayama: Pranayama Dipika*. Aquarian 1992.
Dainin Katigiri, *Returning to Silence*. Shambhala 1988.
Andre van Lysebeth, *Pranayama: Yoga of Breathing*. Thorsons 1979.
Peter Middleton, *The Inward Gaze: Masculinity and Subjectivity in Modern Culture*. Routledge 1992.
Paddy O'Brien, *Self-defence for Everyday*. Sheldon Press 1992.
Sivananda Yoga Group, *The Book of Yoga*. Ebury Press 1983.
Naomi Wolf, *The Beauty Myth: How Images of Beauty are Used Against Women*. Vintage 1991.

Index

abdominal breathing 35–7
abdominals 30–1, 33–4, 60–1
alternate nostril breathing 63–4
anaerobic training 79

cardiovascular fitness 12–16, 47–50, 79–82
chanting 94
commuting 3, 108–11

decision making 1–2
dreams 97–8

eating 8–9, 39–40, 107

fartlek 80–1
fatigue 110–11
flexibility 16–27, 51–7, 83–7

guided fantasy 66–7

health clubs 62, 116
holistic health 1, 7, 13, 39, 70, 98, 107

improved output 2

martial arts 98–9

meditation 94

panic 69, 112–14
pelvic floor exercise 31–2
pollution 13
positive visioning 99–100
pregnancy 4, 114–16

redundancy 116

savasana 37–9
shock 113–14
shoulderstand 55–6
stress management 35–9, 63–9, 90–100
stretching, basic 17–27
support groups 72–3

toning, basic 27–35
training zone 14–15

walking 15
warm-up 28–9

yoga 57, 83

zazen 69